Ready-to-Go
SKILL-BUILDING MATH PACKS
for Independent Learning

Reproducible Packs of
Fun Practice Pages That Help
Kids Really Learn All the Math
Concepts They Need to Know —
Independently!

By Julie Bedora

SCHOLASTIC
PROFESSIONAL BOOKS

New York • Toronto • London • Auckland • Sydney
Mexico City • New Delhi • Hong Kong • Buenos Aires

Dedication

I'd like to dedicate this book to R.S. for motivating me to organize it for publication! It is also dedicated to my parents who have always been unconditionally dedicated to me!

Scholastic, Inc. grants teachers permission to photocopy the activity sheets from this book for classroom use. No other part of this publication may be reproduced in whole or in part, or stored in a retrieval system, or transmitted in any form or by any means, electronic, mechanical, photocopying, recording or otherwise, without written permission of the publisher. For permission, write to Scholastic Professional Books, 555 Broadway, New York, NY 10012-3999.

Developed by Raindrop Publishing LLC
Edited by Lisa Trumbauer
Cover design by James Salerno
Interior design by Debra Spindler
Interior illustration by Laura Rader

ISBN: 0-439-15390-5
Copyright © 2001 by Julie Bedora
All rights reserved.

12 11 10 9 8 7 6 5 4 3 2 1

Table of Contents

Introduction 4

Math Pack 1 11

Math Pack 2 23

Math Pack 3 35

Math Pack 4 49

Math Pack 5 63

Math Pack 6 77

Math Pack 7 93

Math Pack 8 109

Math Pack 9 125

Math Pack 10 141

Math Pack Appendix 157

   Pattern Block Shapes 158

   Student Survey 159

   Student Self-Evaluation 160

   Assessment 161

   End-of-Year Test 162

   End-of-Year Test Answer Key 172

   Square Flashcards 173

   Math Packs Answer Key 181

INTRODUCTION

Welcome to *Ready-to-Go Skill-Building Math Packs for Independent Learning!* These easy-to-use, fun reproducibles are just what you need to get your students excited about math.

You'll find page after page of standards-based addition and subtraction activities, story problems, graphs, shape studies, measurement activities, and so much more! This is just what you need to give your students a head start on building the math skills that will last them a lifetime. At the same time, students will also be strengthening their thinking skills, while mastering the math concepts that will be so important to their success on standardized tests, such as the Terra Nova.

The activities in Math Packs are easy-to-understand and ideal for independent and/or small group learning. The Math Packs have simple, consistent sets of directions that are routinely used throughout each pack. Students spend less time on understanding directions, and more time concentrating on the concept being discovered.

The skill-building activities meet the NCTM Standards and cover a wide range of math concepts:

- **Patterning,** the recognition of number patterns
- **Concept of numbers,** an understanding of counting, ordering, and comparing numbers
- **Computation,** the ability to add, subtract, and estimate quantities
- **Measurement,** the ability to measure length, volume, perimeter, etc.
- **Time,** the ability to tell time to the hour and half hour
- **Money,** the ability to count money and make decisions about wise purchases
- **Geometry,** the study of shapes
- **Data analysis,** the ability to read and create graphs
- **Probability,** an understanding that some events are more likely to happen than others.

HOW TO USE MATH PACKS

Ahead of time, make enough copies of each pack for your class and staple them together. Also be sure to make copies of the Student Self-Evaluation and Assessment page in the Appendix section. You'll need to attach a Student Self-Evaluation to the back of each pack.

When introducing Math Packs, it would be beneficial to quickly walk your students through each activity. You can also let them know that they'll be receiving additional packs to complete throughout the school year. Students will be eager to work through the activities in one pack so they can go on to the next. Show them how to fill out the self-evaluation form. They'll be excited to color in the stars on the bottom to show how well they did. The sequence of activities within each pack is left up to you. You can do them in order or mix them up, whichever best suits your goals or the needs of your class!

MATERIALS NEEDED

Math Packs combine hands-on activities with paper and pencil data recording. The kinds of manipulatives your students will need to have in order to complete some of the activities in this book include:

- **links** (enough for small groups to measure classroom items)
- **measuring cups:** cups, 1/2 cups, 1/3 cups, 1/4 cups, 1/8 cups
- **measuring spoons**: tablespoons, teaspoons, 1/2 tsp., 1/3 tsp., 1/4 tsp., 1/8 tsp.
- **measuring containers**: gallons, quarts, 1/2 gallons
- **measuring tapes**
- **pennies** (10 per child)
- **rulers** (inches/centimeters)
- **pattern blocks** (or reproducible pattern block shapes on page 158)
- **string**
- **tiles**

The number of manipulatives to have on hand depends on how you want to structure the activities. You may want to have some of the activities completed as a whole class, small group, partner, or individualized activity. Look through the activities before handing out each pack. This will help you decide how to proceed. You can also set up a small "Math Packs Station" in your math center. Students can go to this station to pick up the manipulatives they need.

MATH PACK COMPONENTS

Math Pack components introduce all of the basic concepts in math and build on them throughout the year. No concept is left "untouched," even if pack 10 is not completed.

Patterning and Number Concepts
Skill: Recognizing Patterns
Materials needed: None

In the patterning exercises, students will study patterns of 1, 2, 3, 4, and so on. Students are often encouraged to recognize and repeat the pattern, as well as to come up with patterns of their own.

Number Problem
Skill: Addition and Subtraction
Materials needed: None

Students are given addition and subtraction equations and are asked to come up with a story that matches the equation. Students are then asked to draw a picture that goes with their story and to come up with additional equations. In later units students are asked to write about their pictures, too.

Coin-Toss Addition
Skill: Addition
Materials needed: Varying amounts of coins for each student

Here, students will be asked to toss a number of coins, then record how many landed heads up or tails up. They mark the number on the activity sheet, "H" for heads, "T" for tails, and then write an addition equation to show the result of their toss. For example, for Math Pack 4, an equation might read: 3 heads + 1 tail = 4 coins total. This activity will help students recognize equations that equal specific sums.

Heads or Tails
Skill: Probability, Addition
Materials needed: Varying amounts of coins for each student

Beginning with Math Pack 4, students learn about probability with the "Heads or Tails" activity. Like the Coin-Toss Addition, students toss the specified amount of coins. They then find the equation on the chart that matches their toss. They color the squares on the chart, then toss again. They keep going, coloring in the squares to show their tosses. The activity is complete when one whole column has been colored. Students have observed which toss occurred most frequently. It can be fun to involve the entire class, letting them work in small groups, then comparing the results.

Pattern Block Design
Skill: Addition, Creative Thinking
Materials needed: Reproducible sheet on page 158 or real Pattern Blocks

Pattern block activities start in Math Pack 3. The top half of the page displays a sample design that use the appropriate number of pieces. For example, 3 pieces are used in Math Pack 3. A corresponding addition equation is included to show the number and type of pieces involved: If 2 triangles and 1 hexagon were used, the equation would be 2 + 1 = 3. Students are then encouraged to create their own pattern block designs using the same number of pieces.

Number Puzzle
Skill: Number Recognition, Addition
Materials needed: None

This activity has two purposes. First, it reinforces number recognition because boxes are arranged to resemble the chapter's numeral. Second, the activity requires students to add more than two numbers in their heads, without the aid of manipulatives. They must write numbers in the boxes so that each row or column equals the numeral of that Math Pack.

The Classroom Store
Skill: Addition, Money
Materials needed: None (coins optional)

Because not all classes will have an area set up as a "store," the classroom-store activity sheets provide items for sale at set prices. In Math Pack 1, students will see one item for sale for 1 cent. In Math Pack 2, students will see two items for sale at 1 cent, 2 cents, and so on. Students must choose items to buy that equal the specified amount of money. Initially, the task seems simple—one item to be bought for 1 cent. As the Packs progress, the combinations become more complex. Students must write the equation to show the various sums of money they must spend to equal the total amount. Finally, students are asked to color the coins they would use to purchase those items. If possible, you could have coins on hand for students to manipulate, or invite students to bring in spare change from home.

Tile Subtraction
Skill: Subtraction
Materials needed: Tiles

This activity is best done in pairs. Give partners the specified amount of tiles. (For example, if you are working with Math Pack 8, the partners would get 8 tiles.) Ask one partner to hide some tiles behind her or his back. On the activity sheet, the other student colors in the tiles to show the number that is left. The student must then figure out how many tiles are hidden by writing a subtraction equation. For example, if the partner is holding out 3 tiles, the equation would be 8 - 3 = 5. So 5 tiles have been hidden. To confirm, have the partner show the remaining tiles.

Coin-Toss Subtraction
Skill: Subtraction
Materials needed: Varying amount of coins per each student

This activity is similar to Coin-Toss Addition, except that now students will be subtracting. After recording the number of heads and tails thrown, students finish the sentence, "There are _____ (more/fewer) heads than tails." Students are then challenged to write a subtraction equation, starting with the total number tossed, subtracting the heads that landed, and coming up with the number of tails. This activity helps students practice their subtraction skills, and prepares them for solving story problems.

Telling Time
Skill: Time
Materials needed: None

Students are encouraged not only to show that they know how to tell time, but to relate time to their lives. After drawing in the asked-for hour or half hour on the clock, students are asked questions, such as what they do at that time, what time it was an hour ago, etc.

Using a Calculator
Skill: Addition, Subtraction, Using a Calculator
Materials Needed: Calculator

Here, students are presented with basic addition and subtraction problems that focus on numbers they have studied up to that point. Students are then invited to check their answers, using a calculator.

Fractions
Skill: Fractions, Critical Thinking
Materials needed: None

The concept of fractions can often be difficult for young learners to grasp. These pages invite students to color in fractions of pictures. For example, Color 1/4 of the circle, can be found in Math Pack 4. After coloring pieces or shapes, students are asked to color objects in groups. The group, then, has become the "whole" of the fraction: Color 3/4 of the trumpets. Students will see a group of 4 trumpets, and they should color in 3 of them. This activity will help them not only visualize a part of a whole object or group, but to see the actual fraction in writing.

Story Problems
Skill: Problem Solving
Materials needed: None

Each Math Pack also contains a set of "story problems." The story problems challenge students to apply both addition and subtraction skills. At the bottom of each story-problem page, students will find manipulatives that can be cut out. These manipulatives can be placed within the scene at the top of the page, then moved accordingly, to help students solve the problem.

When tackling the story problems, you may find it helpful to guide students through a problem-solving strategy called UPS AL:

1. **U**nderstanding the problem: This calls for students to read the text thoroughly, underline the question, then highlight facts needed to solve the problem.

2. **P**lanning the solution: Students decide if they need to add, subtract, or apply some other math concept.

3. **S**olving the problem: Students are encouraged to use manipulatives, a model, or a picture to help them "see" the problem in order to solve it. They then must write an equation to solve the problem.

4. **A**nswering the question: Students then write the answer in the appropriate space, or in a complete sentence, whichever is asked for.

5. **L**ooking back: The final step reminds students to check their work. Did they use the correct math function? Did they write the equation correctly? Did they solve the equation correctly?

Shape Study
Skill: Identifying Shapes
Materials needed: None

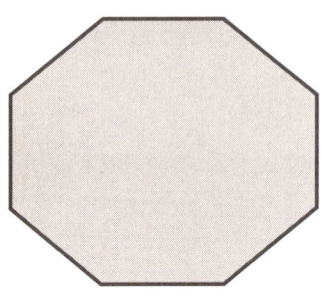

This page introduces students to geometric shapes with varying numbers of sides. After seeing an example of the shape, students are encouraged to draw a different shape with the same amount of sides, using the "geoboards" at the bottom of the page. If possible, you might have them first create their shapes on an actual geoboard with rubber bands, then recreate it on the activity sheet. The letters and numbers along the geoboard's *x* and *y* axes also promote an understanding for how a grid works.

Graphing
Skill: Graphing, Comparing
Materials needed: None

You will find a graphing activity in each Math Pack, with the corresponding number of categories. For example, in Math Pack 3, students will record information in three categories on an overlapping Venn diagram—friends who have cats, families who have dogs, and families who have both. The data is then transferred to a bar graph and discussed. Some of the graphing activities are meant to be done in small groups or as an individual activity.

Measuring Length
Skill: Measuring Length, Counting
Materials needed: Links, Rulers, Measuring Tapes, String

Each of the ten Math Packs introduces students to a different way of measuring length. For example, Math Pack 2 invites students to measure using links. Math Pack 3 asks them to measure with a tape measure. Math Pack 4 encourages students to predict the length, then test their predictions with a ruler.

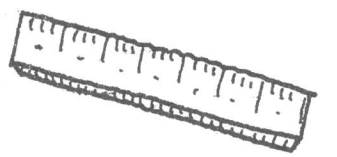

Measuring Perimeter
Skill: Measuring Perimeter
Materials needed: Rulers

These pages will ask students to find the perimeter of varying shapes by measuring and then adding up the sides of each shape.

Measuring Volume
Skill: Measuring Volume, Counting
Materials needed: Measuring Cups (cups, 1/2 cups, 1/3 cups, 1/4 cups, 1/8 cups), Measuring Spoons (tablespoons, teaspoons, 1/2 tsp., 1/3 tsp., 1/4 tsp., 1/8 tsp), Measuring Containers (gallons, quarts, half gallons)

These pages challenge students to learn about measuring volume. Students experiment with gallons, quarts, pints, cups, tablespoons, and teaspoons. And, in a culminating activity in Math Pack 10, students put it all together to follow a recipe.

MATH PACKS APPENDIX

Pattern Block Shapes
On page 158 you will find pattern block shapes that you will need to reproduce once for each student.

Student Survey
A Student Survey is on page 159. This page is fun and easy for students to fill out. Students simply circle or color in the faces to show how they feel about each item listed, such as story problems, making predictions, and even the Math Packs themselves. You can use this survey as an indicator of students' self-confidence and math enjoyment.

Student Self-Evaluation
A student self-evaluation sheet is found on page 160. Encourage students to complete it after they have finished all the Math Pack activities for any given number. Then invite students to color in the stars at the bottom of their page to show how much they've learned!

Assessment
An Assessment sheet is on page 161. You can fill one out for each student after each Math Pack has been completed. You can then keep these Assessment sheets in a portfolio and chart the progress of each student throughout the year.

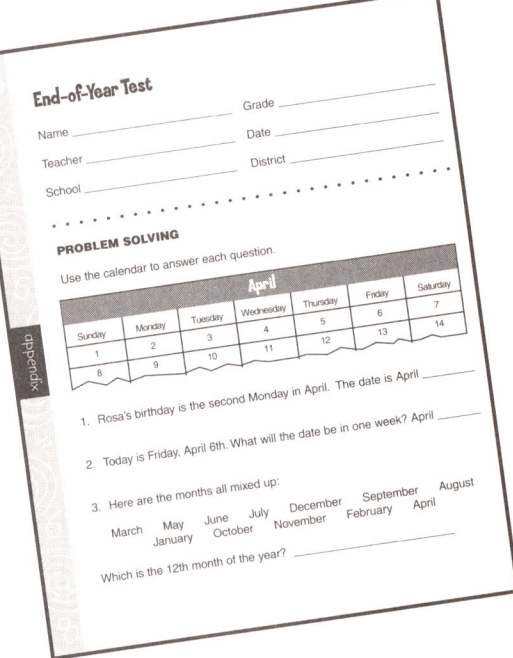

End-of-the-Year Test
Pages 162–171 feature questions to test students' math abilities. Use this test as a pretest and/or a post-test. You'll discover what students have learned or what they will need to practice.

End-of-Year Test Answer Key
Page 172 will supply you with the answers to the test.

Square Flash Cards
The square-shaped flash cards found on pages 173–180 can be used to reinforce addition and subtraction skills. Reproduce the cards for small group activities or as a take-home activity. After reproducing the cards, cut them apart and write the answers to the equations on the back.

Math Packs Answer Key
Pages 181-184 will supply you with the answers for all 10 Math Packs.

Students will be having so much fun completing each Math Pack activity that they won't even realize they're building important math skills at the same time. With *Ready-to-Go Skill-Building Math Packs,* it's easy to create an exciting learning environment for your class!

Math Pack 1

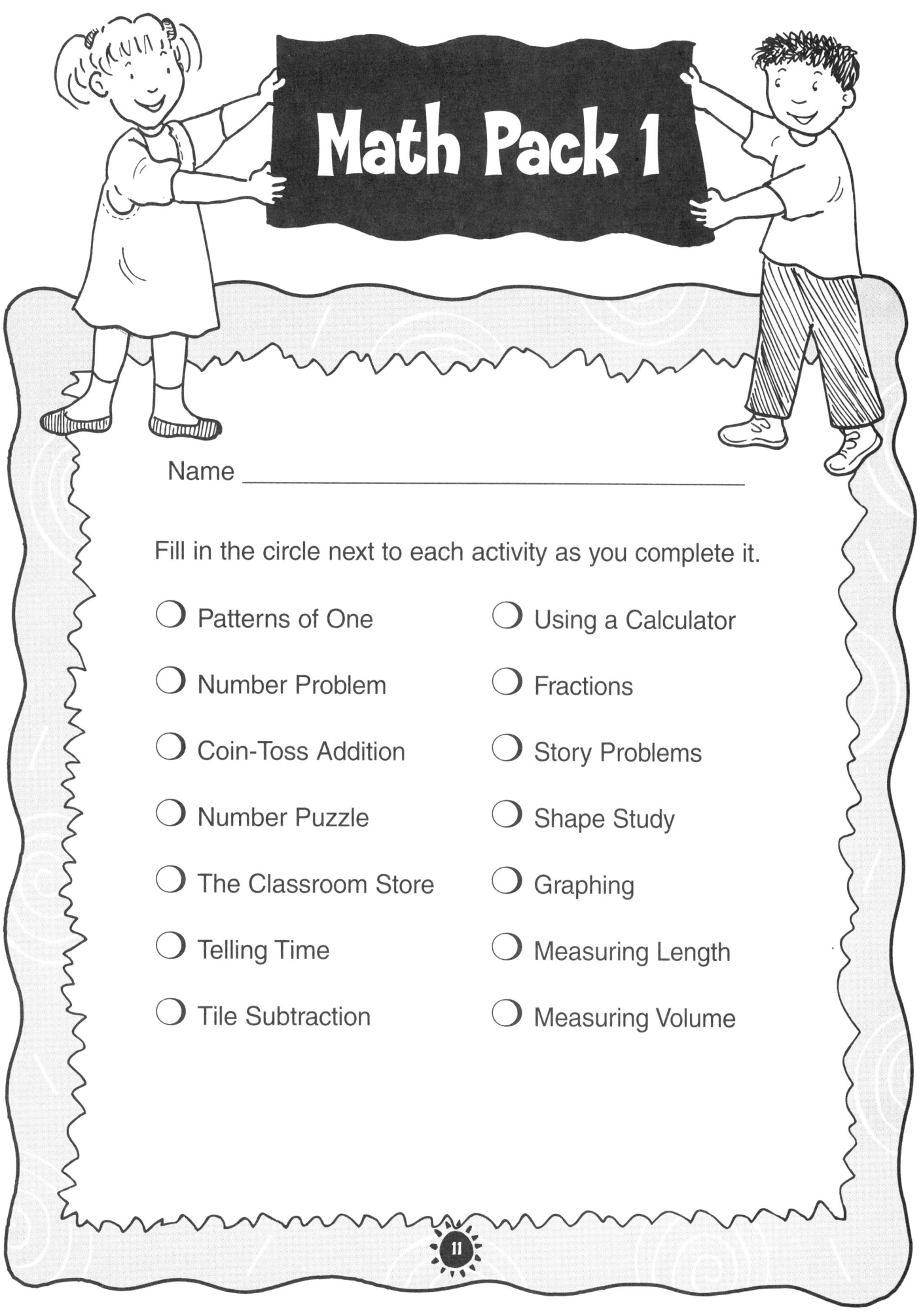

Name _____

Fill in the circle next to each activity as you complete it.

- ○ Patterns of One
- ○ Number Problem
- ○ Coin-Toss Addition
- ○ Number Puzzle
- ○ The Classroom Store
- ○ Telling Time
- ○ Tile Subtraction

- ○ Using a Calculator
- ○ Fractions
- ○ Story Problems
- ○ Shape Study
- ○ Graphing
- ○ Measuring Length
- ○ Measuring Volume

Name _____

Recognizing Patterns

Patterns of One

A pattern is something that keeps repeating exactly the same way. What patterns do you see here? Circle the one that is not a pattern.

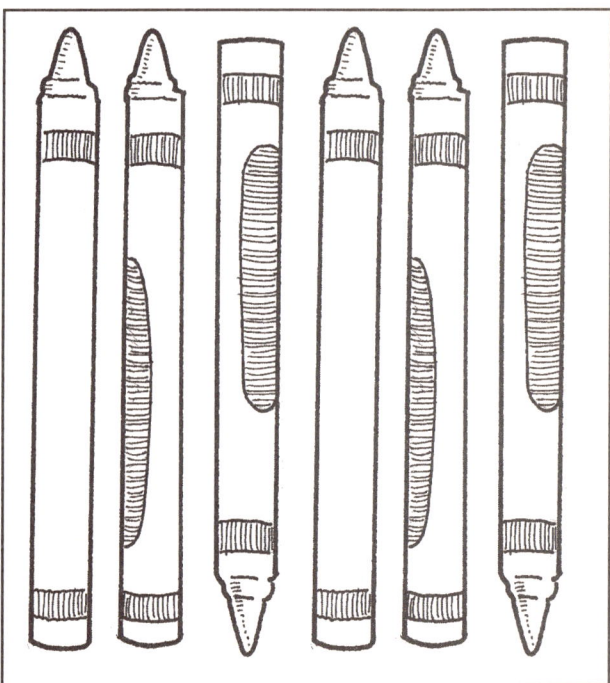

Name _____

Addition

Number Problem

Look at the equation below.

$1 + 0 = 1$

Make up a story to go with the equation.

Draw a picture in the box to go with your story.

Can you think of another equation that makes 1?

Write it on the line below.

Equation: _____

• •

Coin-Toss Addition

Toss one coin. Write "H" for heads or "T" for tails in the circle below to show your toss. Then write an addition equation using 1 and 0. Write the number of "heads" first.

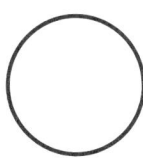

Equation:

_____ + _____ = _____
    H   T

Compare your equation with a classmate's.
Did you both write the same equation? _____

Name _____

Adding, Money

Number Puzzle

These boxes form the number 1.
Write a number in each box.
You can use 0 and 1.
When you add up all the numbers,
the sum should be 1.

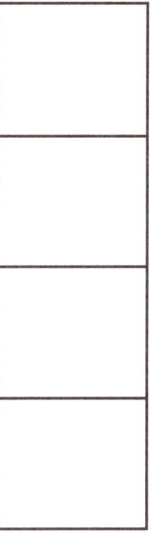

The Classroom Store

Look at what is for sale in the class store.
You have to spend 1¢. Color what you will buy.

Write an equation to show how much you spent.

_____ + _____ = _____

Which coin did you give the clerk? Color it in.

Name _____

Time, Counting

Telling Time

Why do we need to know how to tell time? List your ideas below.

_____

_____

_____

_____

How Long Is a Minute?

Think about how much you can do in one minute.
Write your estimates in the Prediction column. Then time yourself.
Write the actual number in the Result column.

Prediction: In One Minute I Can	Result
Jump rope _____ times.	
Write the numbers from 1 to _____ .	
Say the names of _____ animals.	

Name _____

Subtraction, Addition

Tile Subtraction

Take 1 tile. Have a classmate hide it in his or her hand.
In the tile below, write the number of tiles hidden.
Write a subtraction equation to show how many tiles you have left.

Equation: _____ - _____ = _____

Using a Calculator

Solve the equations below. Check your answers with a calculator.

Add:

0 + 0 = _____   0 + 1 = _____   1 + 0 = _____

Subtract:

1 - 1 = _____   0 - 0 = _____   1 - 0 = _____

Name _____

Critical Thinking

Fractions

A fraction is a part of a whole.

The shapes below are split into parts, or fractions.
Color only the shapes that are split into equal parts (equal fractions).

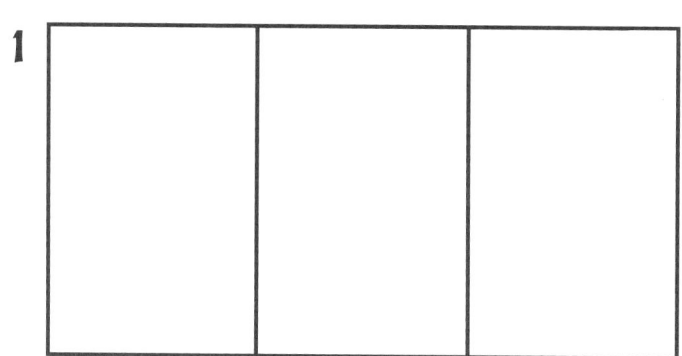
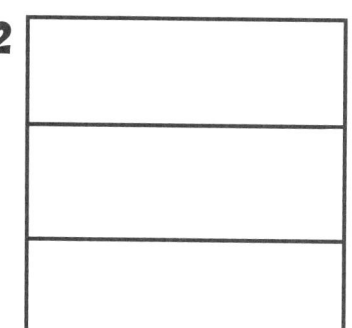
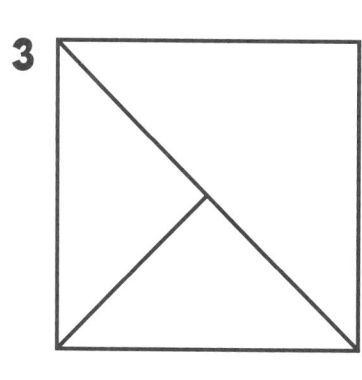
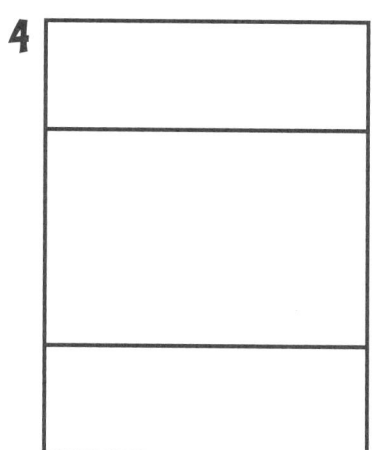
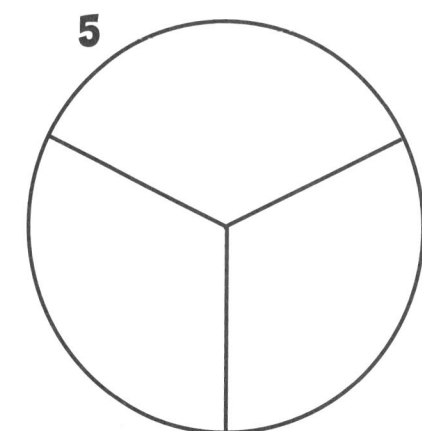
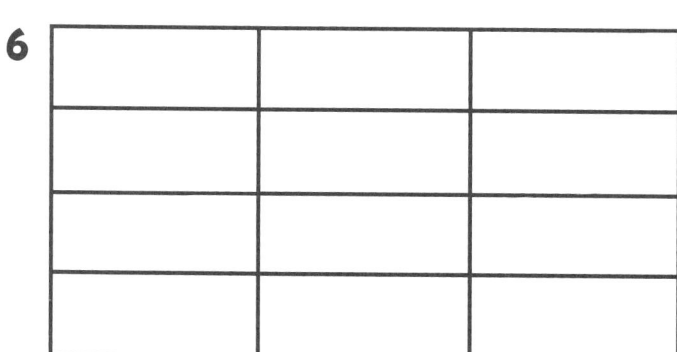
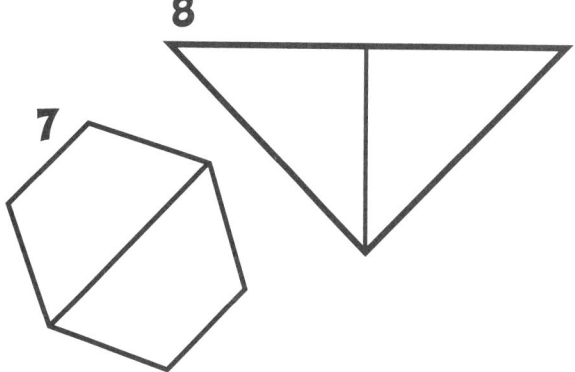

Name _____

Problem Solving

Story Problems

Solve the problems below. Cut out the cherry at the bottom of the page to help you.

1. Lisa made a  .

   She found 1  in a  .

   She <u>did</u> <u>not</u> put it on her  .

   How many 's were left? _____ .

2. Jill made a  .

   She found 1 in a .

   She <u>did</u> put it on her  and ate it.

   How many 's were left? _____ .

Name _____

Shapes, Symmetry

Shape Study

"Symmetry" exists when the two halves of something are mirror images of each other.

Look at the pictures below. Color those that show symmetry.
(Hint: Imagine the pictures are folded on the dotted lines.)

Complete the drawings below. Connect the dots to show the other half.
(Hint: The pictures are symmetrical!)

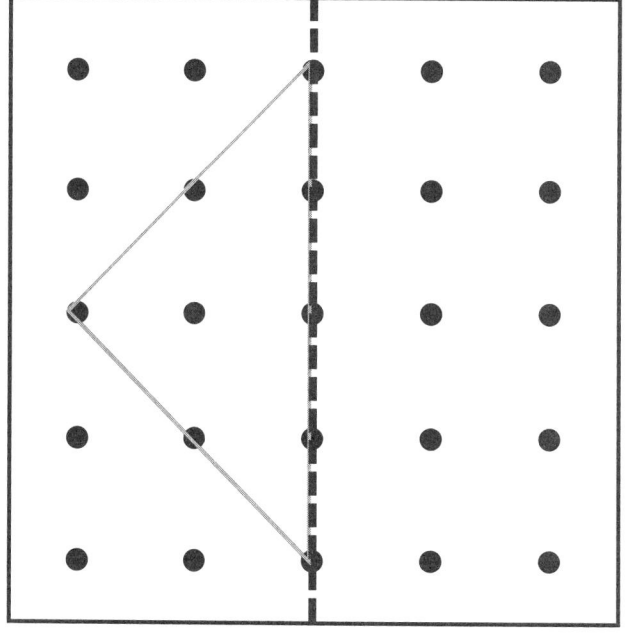
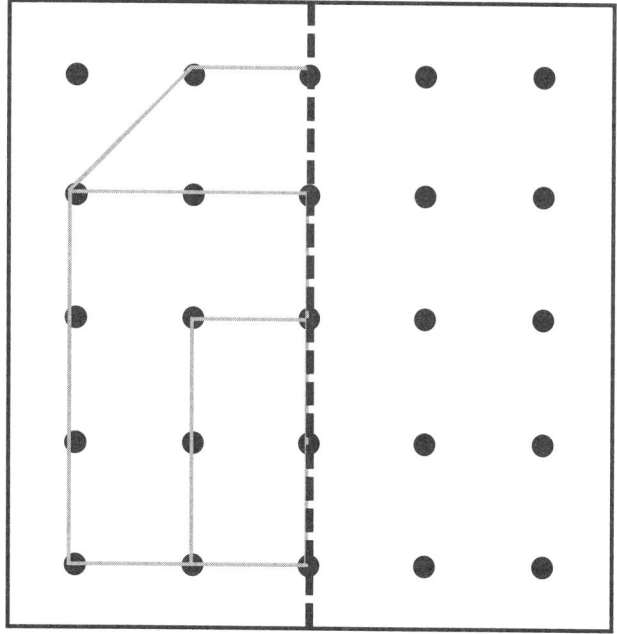

Name _____

Graphing

Graphs can be used to measure many things.
A thermometer is like a graph. It measures heat and cold.

Read the thermometers below. On each line, write the correct temperature.

_____ °F   _____ °F 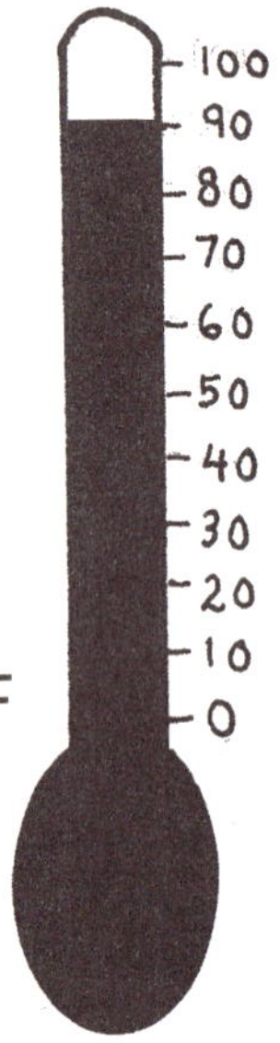   _____ °F 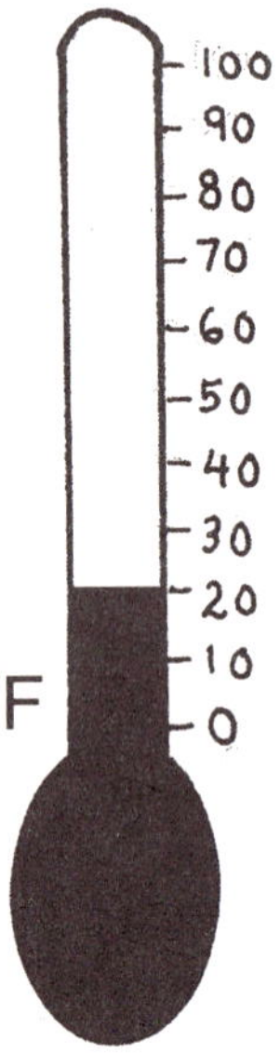   _____ °F

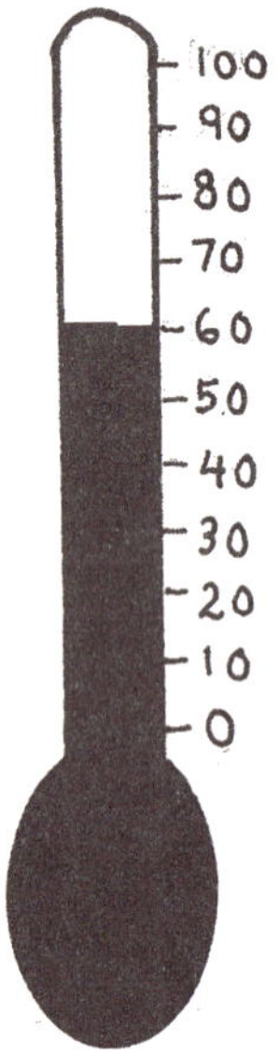

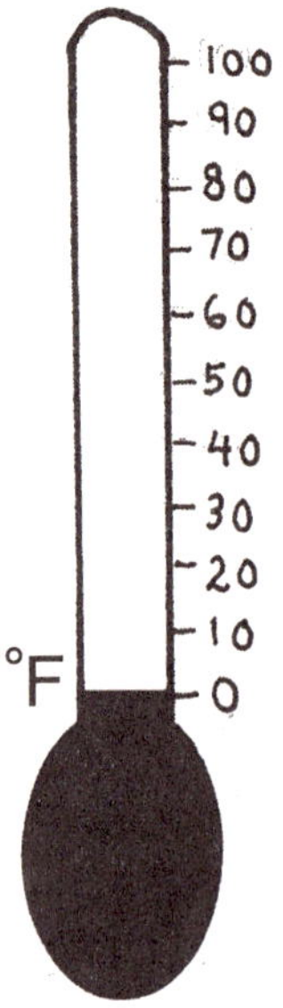

_____ °F 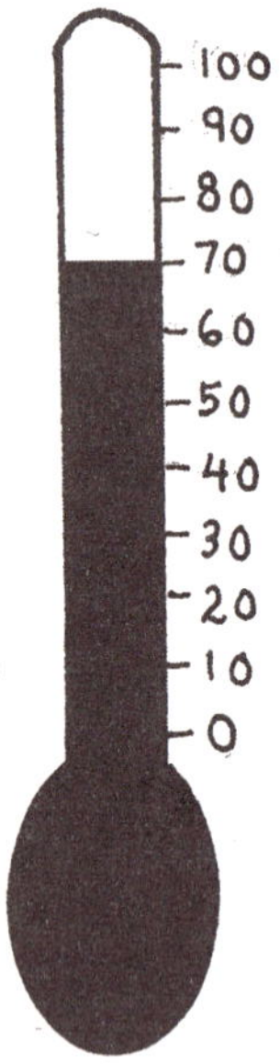   _____ °F 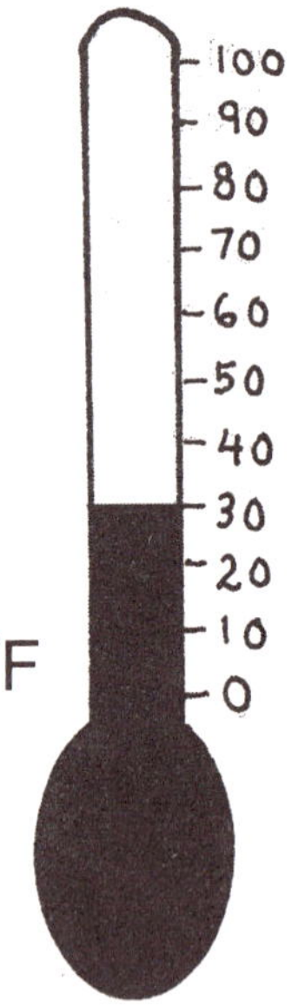   _____ °F 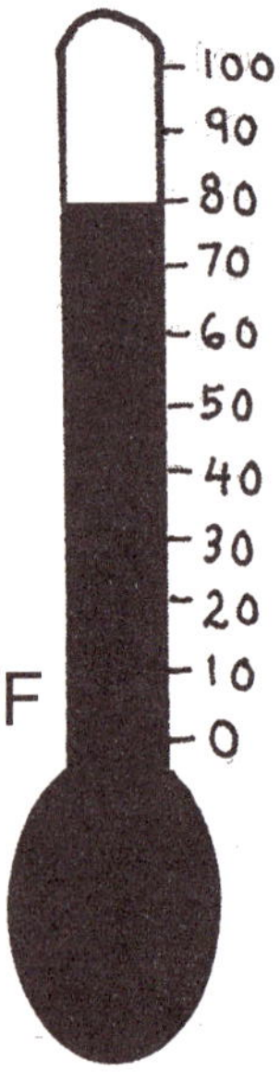   _____ °F

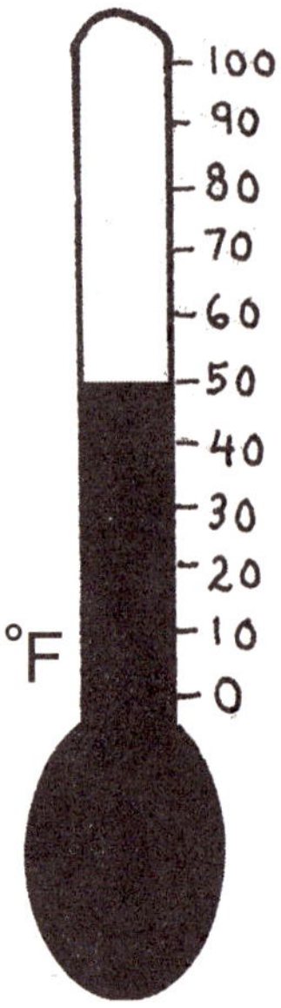

Water freezes at 32°F or below. This is the temperature at which water turns to ice. Circle the thermometers that show temperatures where water would turn to ice.

Name _____

Measuring, Counting

Measuring Length

Work with 5 classmates. Measure some or all of these distances using footsteps.

1. From the  closet to the 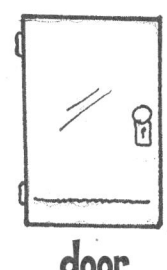 door is _____ footsteps.

2. From the 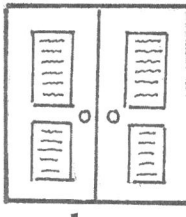 closet to the  chalkboard is _____ footsteps.

3. From the 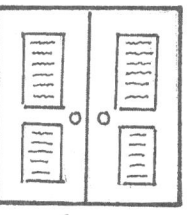 closet to the 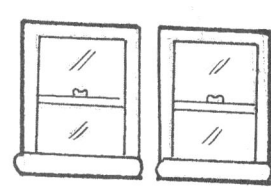 windows is _____ footsteps.

4. From the 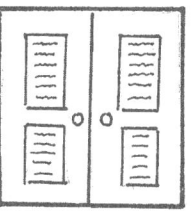 closet to the 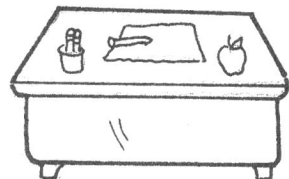 teacher's desk is _____ footsteps.

5. From the 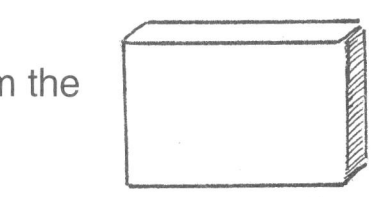 east wall to the  west wall is _____ footsteps.

6. From the 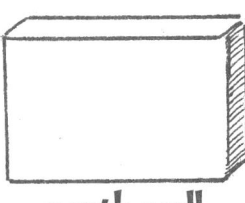 north wall to the  south wall is _____ footsteps.

Name _____

Measuring, Counting

Measuring Volume

How many quarts equal 1 gallon? Find out! Fill a quart container with water. Pour it into a gallon container. Keep doing it until the gallon is full.
Color the correct number of quarts below. Write the numeral on the line.

1 gallon   =   _____ quarts

Now try it with other containers, too.

1 quart   =   _____ pints

1 pint   =   _____ cups

1 cup   =   _____ tablespoons

1 tablespoon   =   _____ teaspoons

Name _____

Recognizing Patterns

Patterns of Two

A pattern can have two things repeating. This is called an "AB" pattern.

1. Look around the classroom. What "AB" patterns do you see? Draw one "AB" pattern in the box.

2. Use a red and blue crayon to color the numbers in the chart using an "AB" pattern.

Hundred's Chart

1	2	3	4	5	6	7	8	9	10
11	12	13	14	15	16	17	18	19	20
21	22	23	24	25	26	27	28	29	30
31	32	33	34	35	36	37	38	39	40
41	42	43	44	45	46	47	48	49	50
51	52	53	54	55	56	57	58	59	60
61	62	63	64	65	66	67	68	69	70
71	72	73	74	75	76	77	78	79	80
81	82	83	84	85	86	87	88	89	90
91	92	93	94	95	96	97	98	99	100

Use this rule:
1 = red
2 = blue
3 = red
4 = blue, and so on.

The blue numbers are even numbers.
They <u>can</u> be split evenly into 2 whole numbers.

The red numbers are odd numbers.
They <u>can not</u> be split evenly into 2 whole numbers.

Name _____

Addition

Number Problem

Look at the equation below.

$1 + 1 = 2$

Make up a story to go with the equation.

Draw a picture in the box to go with your story.

Can you think of another equation that makes 2?

Write it on the line below.

Equation: _____

Coin-Toss Addition

Toss 2 coins. Write "H" for heads or "T" for tails in the circles below to show your toss. Then write an addition equation. Write the number of "heads" first. We did the first one for you!

    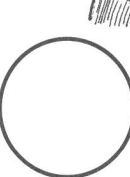

Equation: Equation:

$1 + 1 = 2$

Did you toss the same thing twice? _____
That can happen!

Name _____

Adding, Money

Number Puzzle

These boxes form the number 2.
Write a number in each box.
You can use the numbers 0, 1, or 2.
The sum of each row should equal 2.
The sum of each column should equal 2.

The Classroom Store

Look at what is for sale in your class store. You have to spend 2¢. You should only buy 1 thing. Color what you will buy.

1¢

2¢

Write an equation to show how much you spent.

_____ + _____ = _____

Which coins did you give the clerk? Color them in.

Name _____

Time

Telling Time

Draw the hands on the clock so it shows 2:00.

Draw the hands on the clock so it shows 3:00.

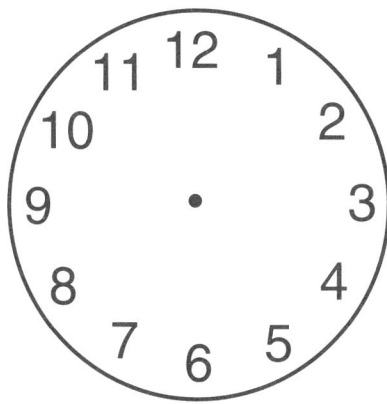

Draw the hands on the clock so it shows 4:00.

Draw the hands on the clock so it shows 5:00.

What do you do at 2:00? Write it on the lines below.

_____

_____

Name _____

Subtraction, Addition

Tile Subtraction

Take 2 tiles. Have a classmate hide 1, 2, or no tiles in his or her hand. Color in the tiles below to show how many are left. Write a subtraction equation to show how many tiles your classmate is hiding. We did the first one for you.

Equation: __2 – 1 = 1__   Equation: _____

Using a Calculator

Solve the equations below.
Check your answers with a calculator.

Add:

1 + 1 = ____   2 + 0 = ____   0 + 1 = ____   0 + 1 = ____

Subtract:

2 – 2 = ____   2 – 1 = ____   1 – 1 = ____   2 – 0 = ____

Name _____

Fractions, Critical Thinking

Fractions

Something that is split in 2 equal parts is divided in "half."

These two shapes are divided in half.

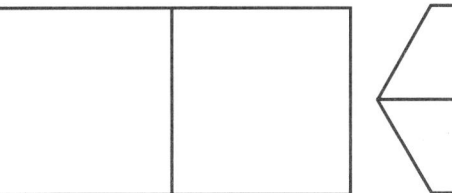

A fraction has a number on the top: ⟶ $\frac{1}{2}$

A fraction has a number on the bottom, too: ⟶

The top number tells the "fraction," or parts, of the whole.
The bottom number tells the number of parts in the whole.

Draw a line to match the picture with a fraction.

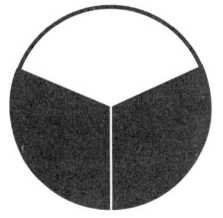  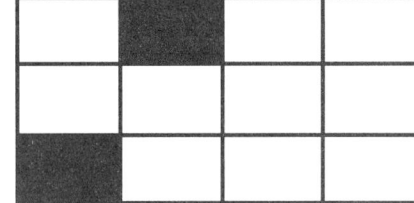

$\frac{2}{2}$ $\frac{2}{12}$ $\frac{2}{3}$

The top number in these fractions tells you how many parts to color. Try it!

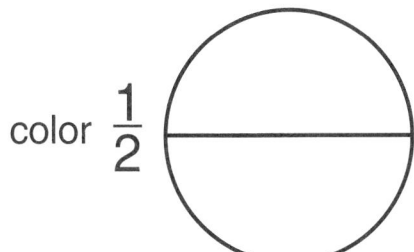 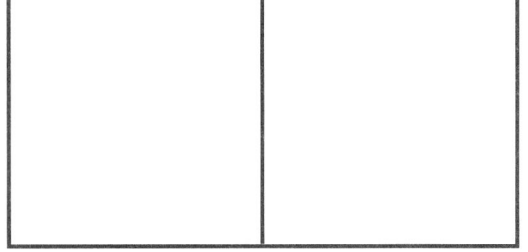

color $\frac{1}{2}$ color $\frac{2}{2}$

Name _____

Problem Solving

Story Problems

Solve these story problems. Cut out the drumsticks at the bottom of the page to help you.

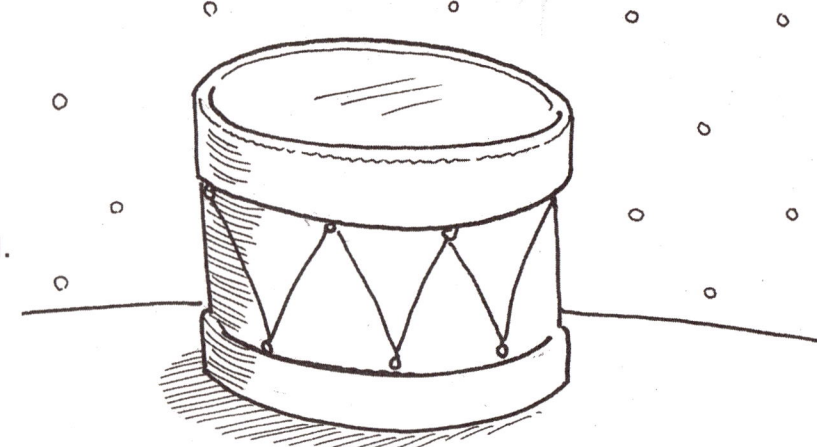

1. Kiley had a with 2

   1  broke.

   How many were left? _____

2. Michael had a  with 2  .

   1  was blue.

   1  was red.

   How many did Michael have? _____

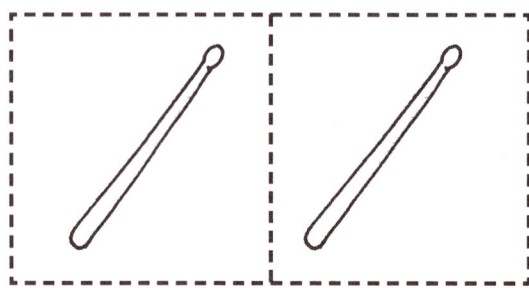

Name _____

Identifying Shapes

Shape Study

Circle

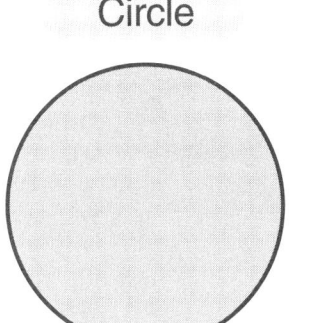

A circle has 0 sides.

Oval

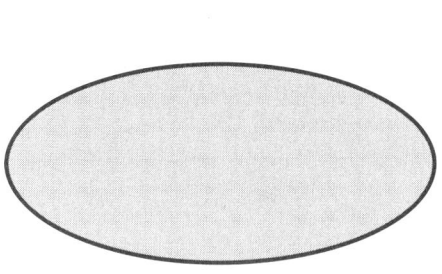

An oval has 0 sides.

Try to connect the dots in the geoboards below to make shapes with 0 sides.

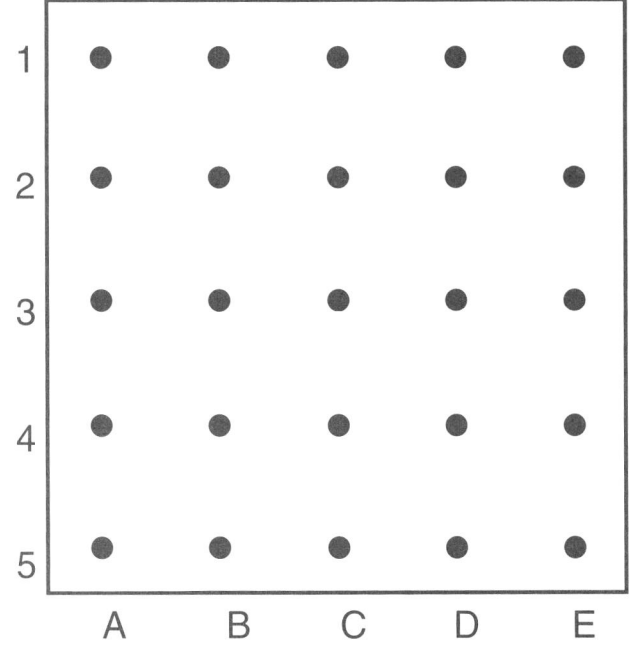
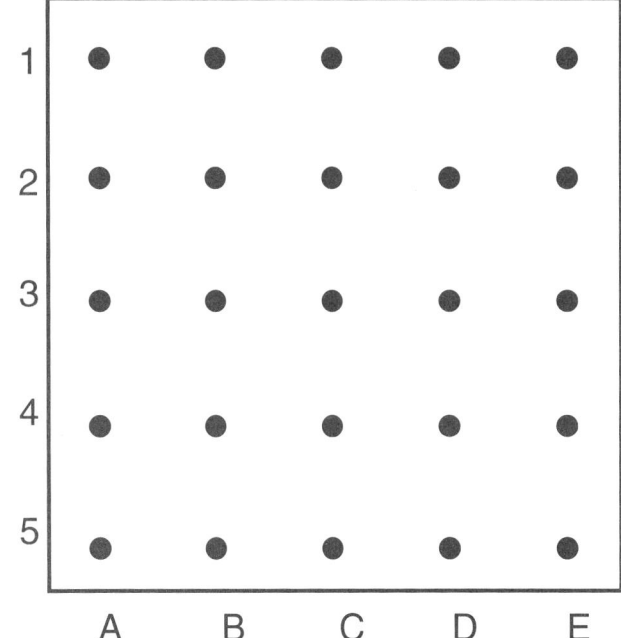

Were you able to do it? Why or why not?

_____

_____

Name _____

Graphing, Comparing

Sorting and Graphing

Sort the students in your class.
Put a tally mark for each boy and each girl in the correct circle below.

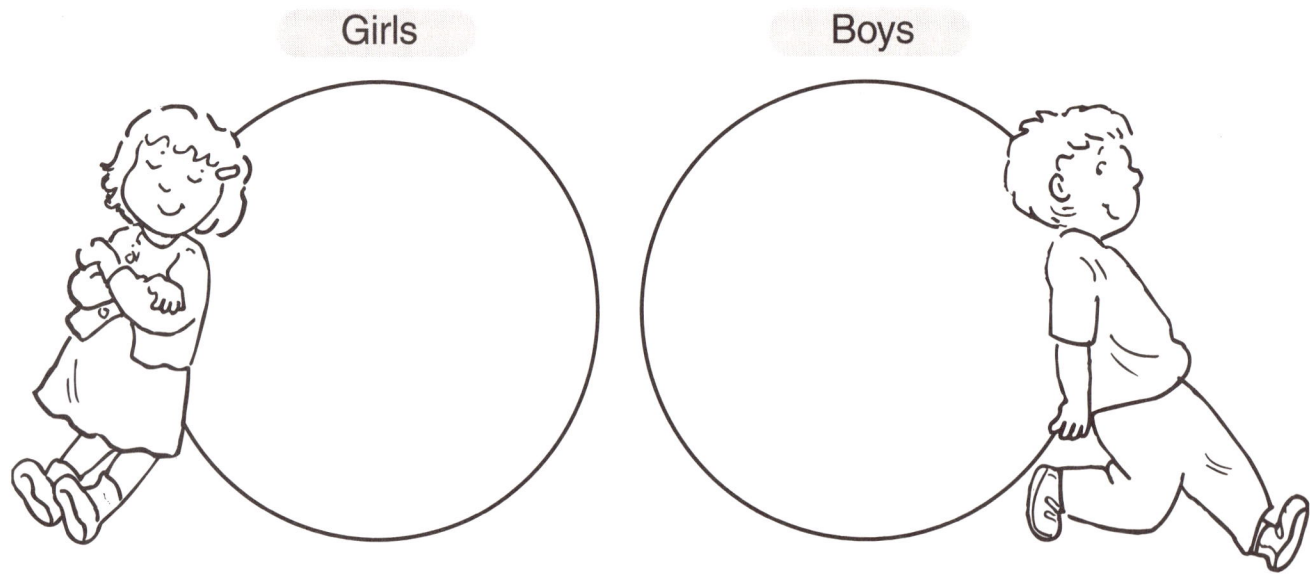

Now fill in the graph. Color in 1 square for each tally mark.

Girls
Boys

Look at the graph. Try not to count!

Does your class have more girls or boys? _____

How can you tell? _____

Now count them: Girls _____   Boys _____

Were you right? _____

How many students are in your class? _____

Name _____

Measuring, Counting

Measuring Length

Work with a partner. Measure these items in your classroom using links.

door _____ links

chair _____ links

window _____ links

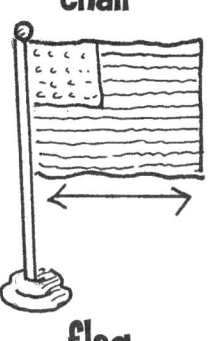
flag _____ links

teacher's desk _____ links

trash can _____ links

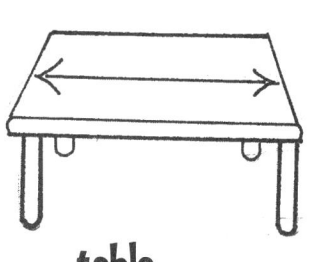
table _____ links

arm _____ links

Name _____

Measuring, Fractions

Measuring Volume

Predict how many 1/2 gallons fill 1 gallon. Try it! Then color the correct amount.

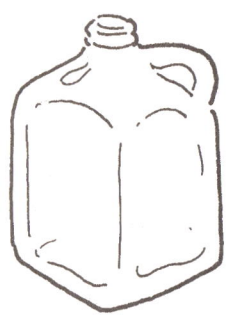 

1 gallon = _____ 1/2 gallons

Draw something you can buy in a 1/2 gallon.

Predict how many 1/2 cups fill 1 cup. Try it! Then color in the correct amount.

1 cup = _____ 1/2 cups

Draw something you can measure by the 1/2 cup.

Predict how many 1/2 teaspoons fill 1 teaspoon. Try it! Then color in the correct amount.

 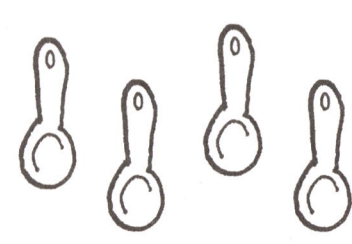

1 teaspoon = _____ 1/2 teaspoons

Draw something you can measure by the 1/2 teaspoon.

Math Pack 3

Name _____

Fill in the circle next to each activity as you complete it.

- ○ Patterns of Three
- ○ Number Problem
- ○ Coin-Toss Addition
- ○ Pattern Block Design
- ○ Number Puzzle
- ○ The Classroom Store
- ○ Tile Subtraction
- ○ Using a Calculator

- ○ Coin-Toss Subtraction
- ○ Fractions
- ○ Story Problems
- ○ Shape Study
- ○ Telling TIme
- ○ Sorting and Graphing
- ○ Measuring Length
- ○ Measuring Volume

Name _____

Recognizing Patterns

Patterns of Three

1. A pattern can have 3 things repeating. Write in a letter for each animal. Make sure you repeat the same letter for the same animal.

_____ _____ _____ _____ _____ _____

_____ _____ _____ _____ _____ _____

_____ _____ _____ _____ _____ _____

2. Make a pattern of these three sounds: Clap, snap, or slap your knees. For example: clap, clap, slap/clap, clap, slap.

_____ _____ _____ _____

_____ _____ _____ _____

Ask a classmate to repeat your sound pattern.

3. Arrange some crayons in a pattern of three. Ask a classmate to continue the pattern.

Name _____

Addition

Number Problem

Look at the equation below.

2 + 1 = 3

Make up a story to go with the equation.

Draw a picture in the box to go with your story.

Can you think of another equation that makes 3?

Write it on the line below.

Equation: _____

Coin-Toss Addition

Toss 3 coins. Write "H" for heads or "T" for tails in the circles below to show your toss. Then write an addition equation. Write the number of "heads" first. We did the first one for you!

Equation:

_____ 1 + 2 = 3 _____

 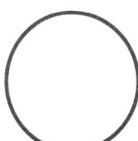 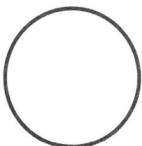

Equation:

_____

Name _____

Creative Thinking

Pattern Block Design

How many total pieces are in this pattern block design?

2 + 1 = _____

Now make your own design. Use 3 pattern blocks from the pattern block page. Cut out the shapes and trace or glue them in the space below. You may need to use a shape more than once.

Write an equation to show how many of each shape you used.

Equation: _____

Name _____

Adding, Money

Number Puzzle

These boxes form the number 3.
Write a number in each box.
You can use 0, 1, 2, or 3.
The sum of each row should equal 3.
The sum of each column should equal 3.

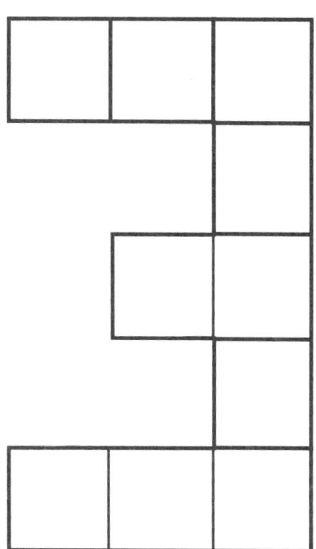

The Classroom Store

Look at what is for sale in the class store. You have to spend 3¢. What will you buy? You should only buy 1 thing or 2 things. Color what you will buy.

1¢    2¢ 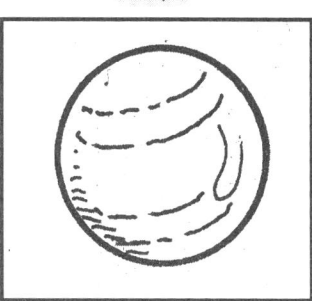   3¢

Write an equation to show how much you spent.

_____

Which coins did you give the store clerk? Color them in.

Name _____

Subtraction, Addition

Tile Subtraction

Take 3 tiles. Ask a classmate to hide some in his or her hand.
Color in the tiles below to show how many are left.
Write a subtraction equation to find out how many tiles
your classmate is hiding. We did the first one for you.

Equation: __3 – 2 = 1__   Equation: _____

Equation: _____   Equation: _____

Using a Calculator

Solve the equations below. Check your answers with a calculator.

Add:

0 + 3 = _____   2 + 1 = _____   1 + 1 = _____   2 + 1 = _____

Subtract:

3 - 3 = _____   3 - 2 = _____   3 - 0 = _____   3 - 1 = _____

Name _____

Subtracting 3

Coin-Toss Subtraction

Toss 3 coins. Write "H" for heads or "T" for tails in the circles below to show how the coins landed. Then finish each sentence to tell about your toss. Write a subtraction equation to show your toss, too. Write the number of heads first. We did the first one for you. Try it three times.

"H"=Heads   "T"=Tails

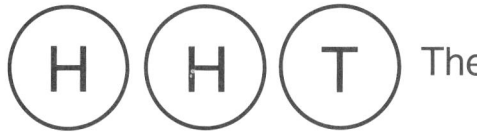 There are ___more___ heads than tails.
(more/fewer)

Subtraction equation: ___3 coins___ - ___2 heads___ = ___1 tail___

◯ ◯ ◯   There are _____ heads than tails.
(more/fewer)

Subtraction equation: _____ - _____ = _____

◯ ◯ ◯   There are _____ heads than tails.
(more/fewer)

Subtraction equation: _____ - _____ = _____

◯ ◯ ◯   There are _____ heads than tails.
(more/fewer)

Subtraction equation: _____ - _____ = _____

Name _____

Fractions, Critical Thinking

Fractions

A fraction has two numbers. The top number will tell you how many parts to color. The bottom number tells you how many parts there are.

Color 1/3 of the triangle.

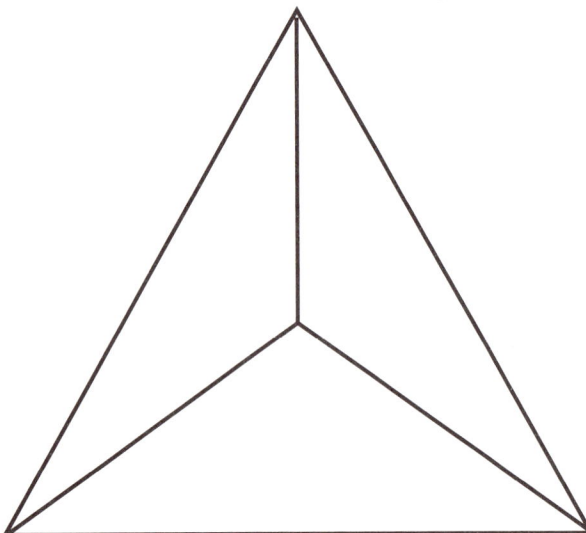

Color 2/3 of the circle.

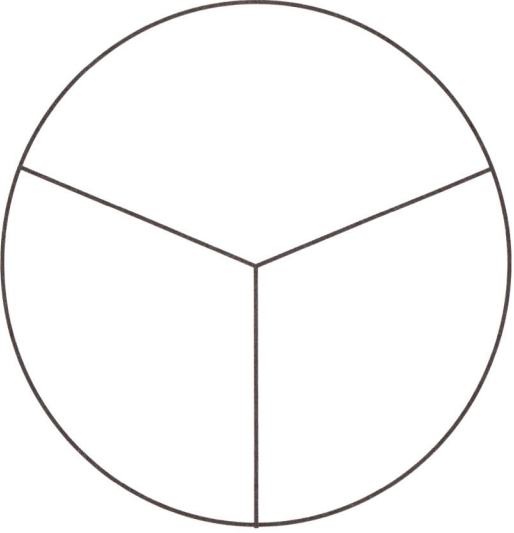

Color 2/3 of the fish.

Color 0/3 of the baseballs.

Color 1/3 of the apples.

Color 3/3 of the turtles.

Name _____

Problem Solving

Story Problems

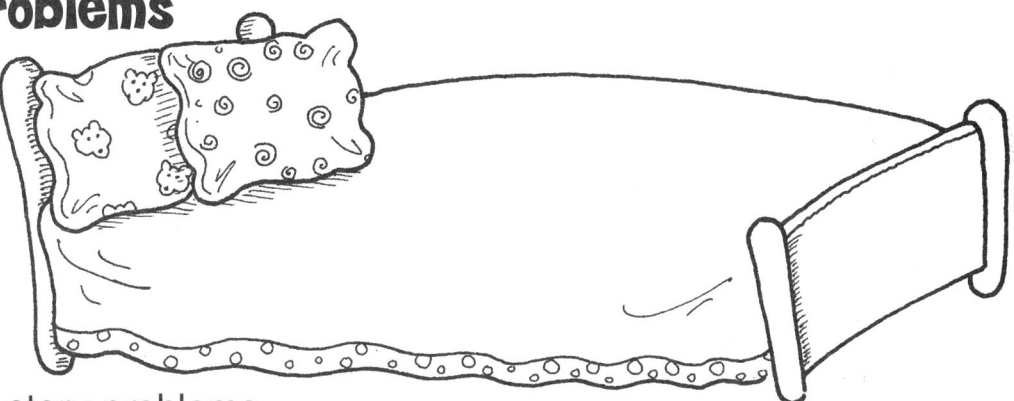

Solve these story problems.
Cut out the teddy bears at the bottom of the page to help you.

1. 3 teddy bears were on Jane's bed.
   Her sister Eva borrowed 2.

   How many teddy bears were left? _____

2. Jonathan didn't have any teddy bears.
   His brother Jackson gave him 2.
   His sister Shannon gave him 1.

   How many teddy bears did Jonathan have then? _____

3. Jimmy had 3 teddy bears.
   He thought he was too old for teddy bears,
   so he gave them all away.

   How many teddy bears did Jimmy have then? _____

Name _____

Identifying Shapes

Shape Study

A triangle has 3 sides.

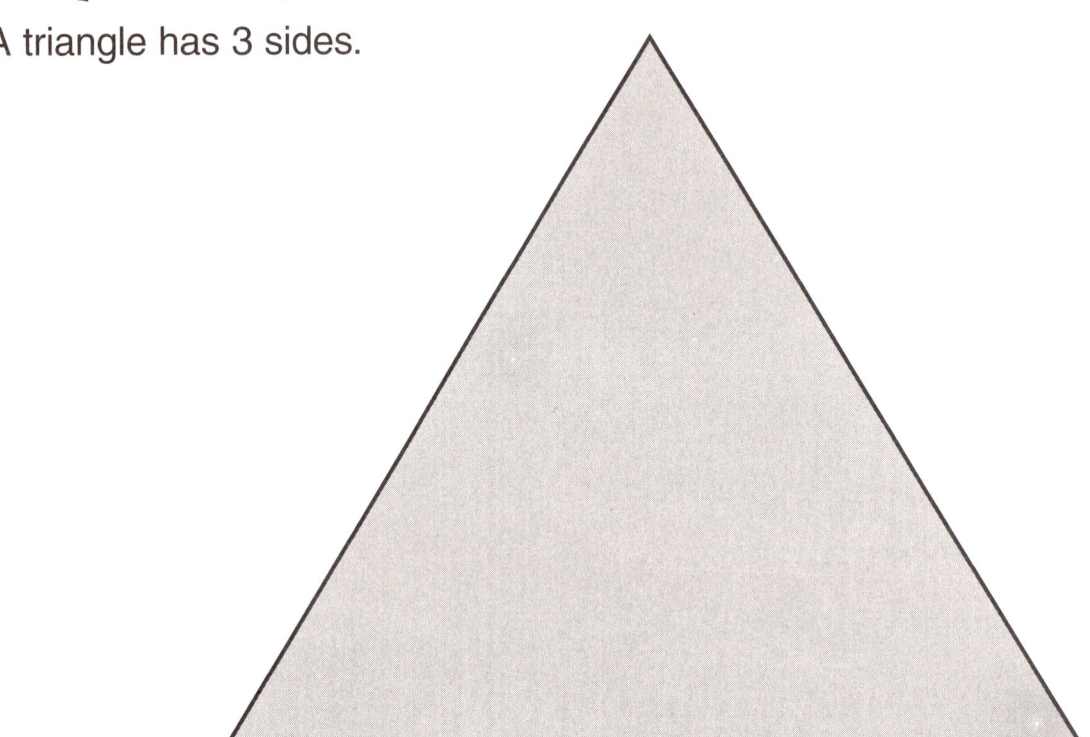

Connect the dots in the geoboards below to make triangles with 3 sides.

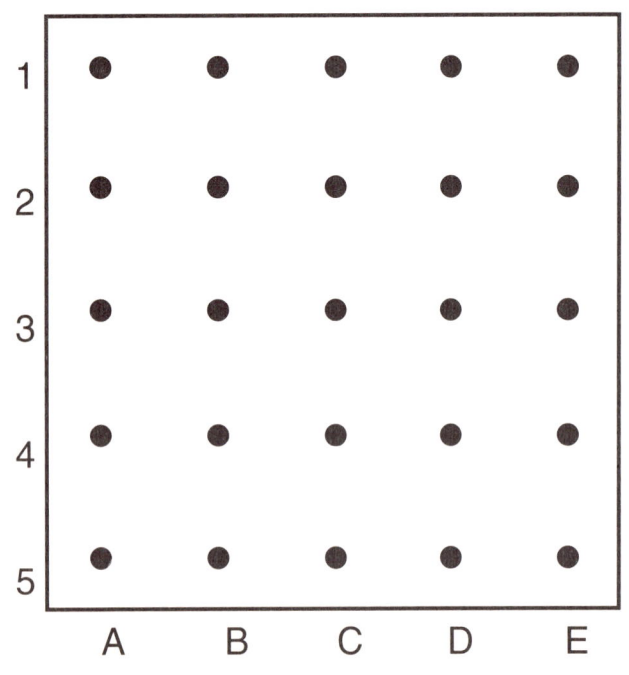
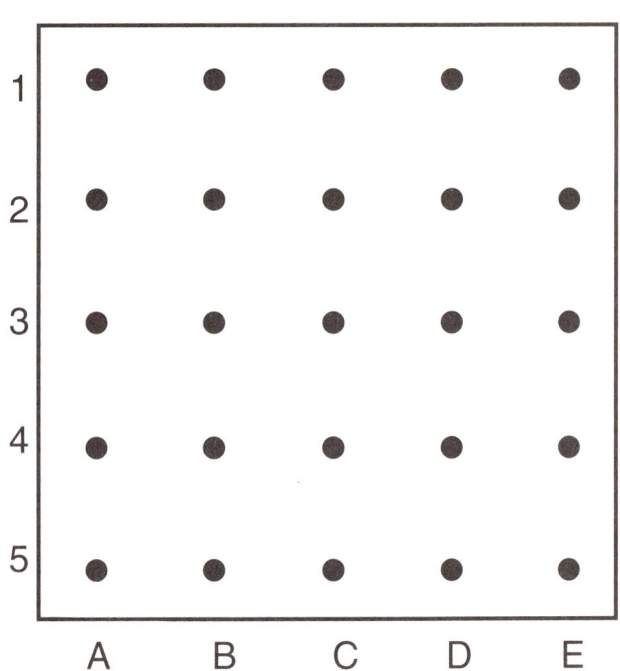

Telling Time

Draw the hands on the clock so it shows 3:00

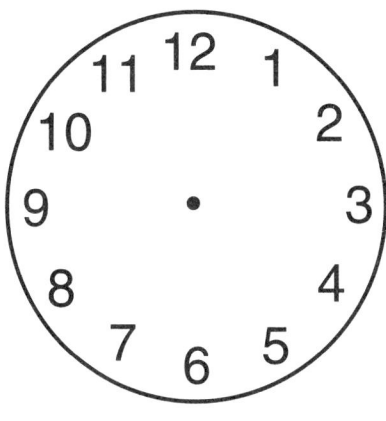

Draw the hands on the clock so it shows 6:00

Draw the hands on the clock so it shows 9:00

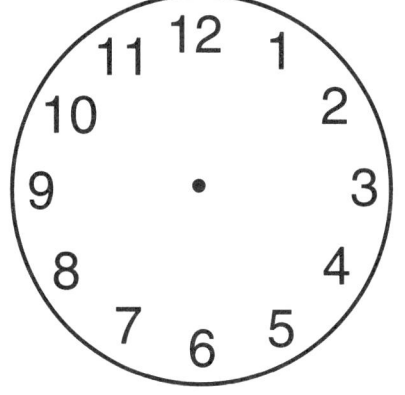

Draw the hands on the clock so it shows 12:00

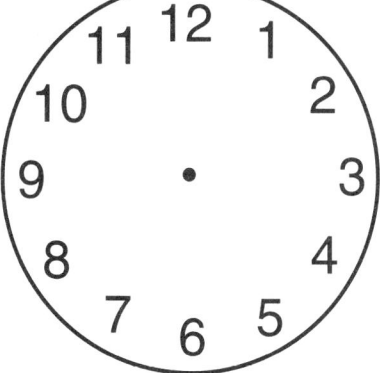

What do you do at 3:00? Write about it on the lines below.

_____

_____

Name _____

Graphing

Sorting and Graphing

Ask 9 friends to help you find out which pet is more popular—cats, dogs, or neither.

1. If you have a cat, draw an X in the "cat" circle.

2. If you have a dog, draw an X in the "dog" circle.

3. If you have a cat and a dog, draw an X where the circles overlap.

4. If you don't have a cat or a dog, draw an X outside the circles.

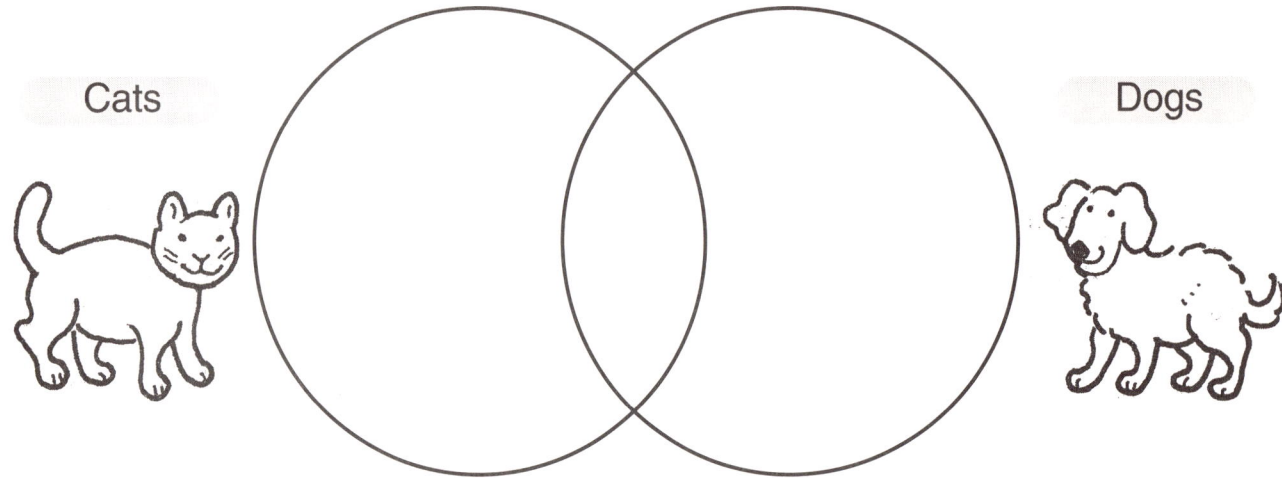

Now fill in the bar graph. Color in 1 square for each X.

Cats										
Dogs										
Both										
Neither										

Look at the graph. Which animal is most popular? _____

How many classmates have both cats and dogs? _____

How many classmates have neither cats nor dogs? _____

Name _____

Measuring Length

Measuring Length

Work with a partner. Measure these items in your classroom using a tape measure.

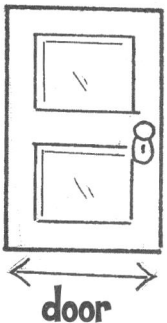
door _____ inches

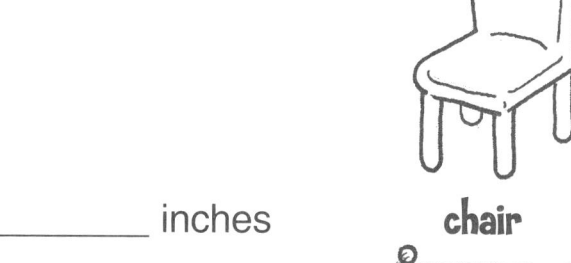
chair _____ inches

window _____ inches

flag _____ inches

teacher's desk _____ inches

trash can _____ inches

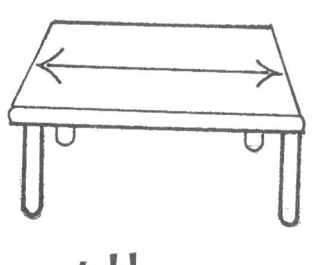
table _____ inches

arm _____ inches

Why does a tape measure work better than a ruler to measure the trash can? Explain your answer on the back.

Name _____

Measuring Volume

Measuring Volume

How many teaspoons of water fill 1 tablespoon? Write your prediction: _____
Try it! Then color the correct amount.

 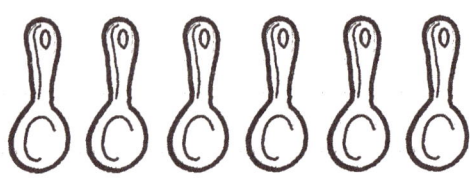

1 tablespoon   =   _____ teaspoons

• •

How many 1/3 cups of water fill 1 cup? Write your prediction: _____
Try it! Then color the correct amount.

1 cup   =   _____ 1/3 cups

• •

Suppose you are making a recipe. You have to measure the ingredients below. Which measuring tool would work the best? If you would use a cup, color the ingredient red. If you would use a teaspoon, color the ingredient blue.

Explain your answers on the back.

Math Pack 4

Name _____

Fill in the circle next to each activity as you complete it.

- ○ Patterns of Four
- ○ Number Problem
- ○ Coin-Toss Addition
- ○ Heads or Tails?
- ○ Pattern Block Design
- ○ Number Puzzle
- ○ The Classroom Store
- ○ Tile Subtraction

- ○ Coin-Toss Subtraction
- ○ Telling Time
- ○ Using a Calculator
- ○ Fractions
- ○ Story Problems
- ○ Shape Study
- ○ Graphing
- ○ Measuring Length
- ○ Measuring Volume

Name _____   **Recognizing Patterns**

Patterns of Four

1. A pattern can have 4 things repeating. Write a letter for each picture. Make sure you repeat the same letter for the same picture.

2. How many seasons are in a year? _____
   The seasons are a pattern of four. They repeat each year. Write the names of the seasons in order on the lines above the boxes. Inside each box, draw a picture to show the correct season.

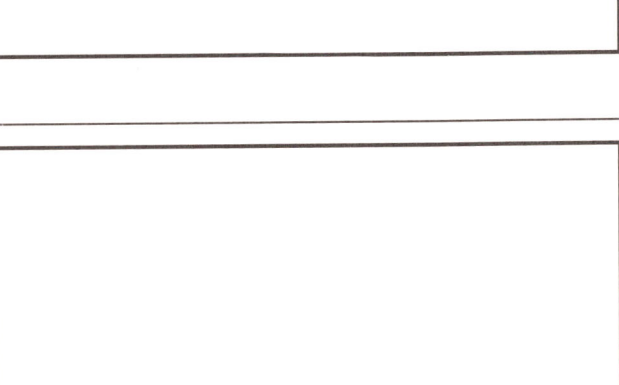

Name _____

Addition

Number Problem

Look at the equation below.

   2 + 2 = 4

Make up a story to go with the equation.

Draw a picture in the box to go with your story.

Can you think of another equation that makes 4?

Write it on the line below.

Equation: _____

- -

Coin-Toss Addition

Toss 4 coins. Write "H" for heads or "T" for tails in the circles below to show your toss. Then write an addition equation. Write the number of "heads" first. We did the first one for you! Try it three times.

(H) (H) (T) (T)   ( ) ( ) ( ) ( )

Equation: __2 + 2 = 4__   Equation: _____

( ) ( ) ( ) ( )   ( ) ( ) ( ) ( )

Equation: _____   Equation: _____

Name _____

Heads or Tails?

Toss 4 pennies. Look at how the coins landed. Which equation below does it match? Color in the lowest box on the chart in the column for that equation. Toss 4 pennies again and again until one whole column has been colored. This is the combination of coins you tossed the most.

0¢ + 4¢   1¢ + 3¢   2¢ + 2¢   3¢ + 1¢   4¢ + 0¢
head tails   heads tails   heads tails   heads tails   heads tails

Probability, Adding

Name _____

Creative Thinking

Pattern Block Design

How many total pieces are in this pattern block design?

1 + 3 = _____

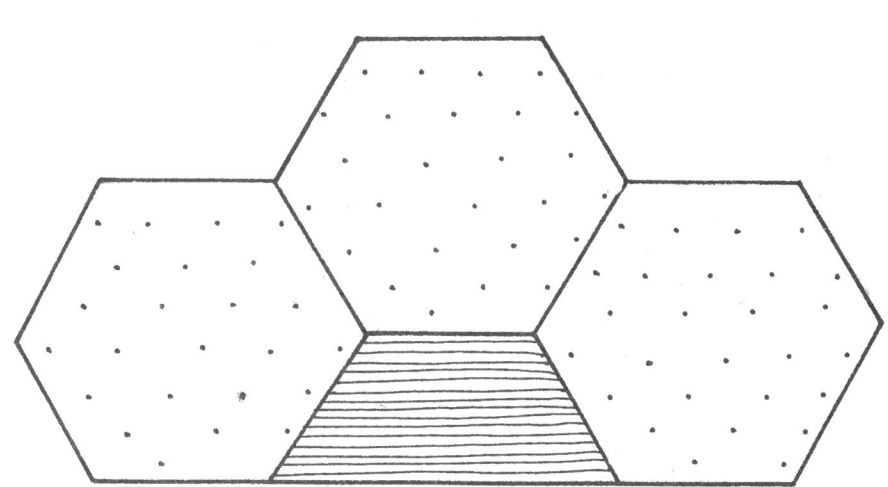

Now make your own design. Use 4 pattern blocks from the pattern block page. Cut out the shapes and trace or glue them in the space below. You may need to use a shape more than once.

Write an equation to show how many of each shape you used.

Equation: _____

Name _____

Adding, Money

Number Puzzle

These boxes form the number 4.
Write a number in each box.
you can use 0, 1, 2, 3, or 4.
The sum of each row should equal 4.
The sum of each column should equal 4.

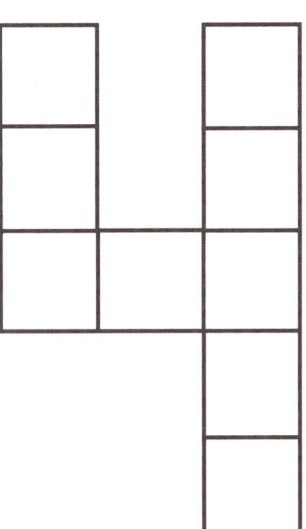

The Classroom Store

Look at what is for sale in the class store. You have to spend 4¢. You should only buy 1 thing or 2 things. Color what you will buy.

1¢    2¢    3¢    4¢

Write an equation to show how much you spent.

_____

Which coins did you give the store clerk? Color them in.

Name _____

Subtracting 4

Tile Subtraction

Toss 4 tiles. Ask a classmate to hide some in his or her hand. Color in tiles below to show how many are left. Write a subtraction equation to find out how many tiles your classmate is hiding. We did the first one for you.

   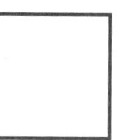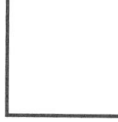

Equation: __4 – 2 = 2__   Equation: _____

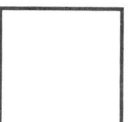   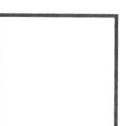

Equation: _____   Equation: _____

• •

Coin-Toss Subtraction

Toss 4 coins. Write "H" for heads or "T" for tails in the circles below to show how the coins landed. Then finish the sentence to tell about your toss. Write a subtraction equation to show your toss, too. Write the number of heads first. For example: 4 coins - 2 heads = 2 tails.

"H"=Heads   "T"=Tails

There are _____ heads than tails.
          (more/fewer)

Subtraction equation: _____ - _____ = _____

Name _____

Time, Calculator

Telling Time

What time is 4:00?
Draw it on the clock.

What time is 4:30?
Draw it on the clock.

What do you do at 4:00? Write about it on the lines below.

_____

_____

• •

Using a Calculator

Solve the equations below. Check your answers with a calculator.

Add:

Subtract:

4 + 0 = _____   2 + 2 = _____   4 - 3 = _____   4 - 2 = _____

2 + 1 = _____   3 + 1 = _____   4 - 0 = _____   3 - 2 = _____

1 + 3 = _____   0 + 0 = _____   2 - 1 = _____   4 - 1 = _____

Name _____

Fractions, Critical Thinking

Fractions

A fraction has two numbers. The top number will tell you how many parts to color. The bottom number tells you how many parts there are.

Color 1/4 of the circle.

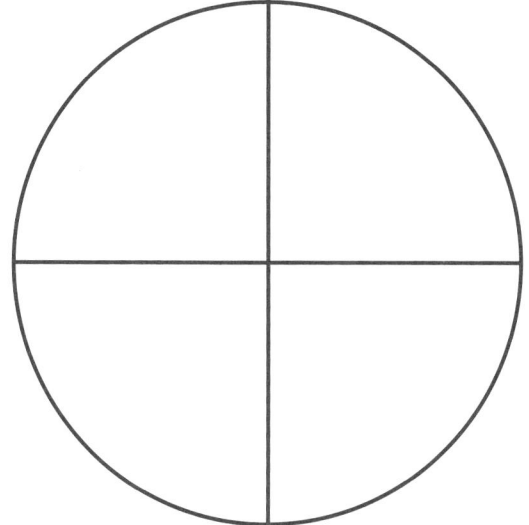

Color 2/4 of the triangle.

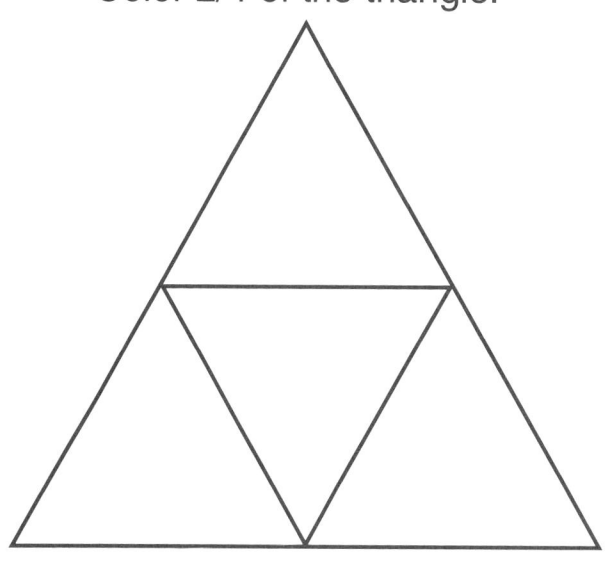

Color 3/4 of the trumpets.

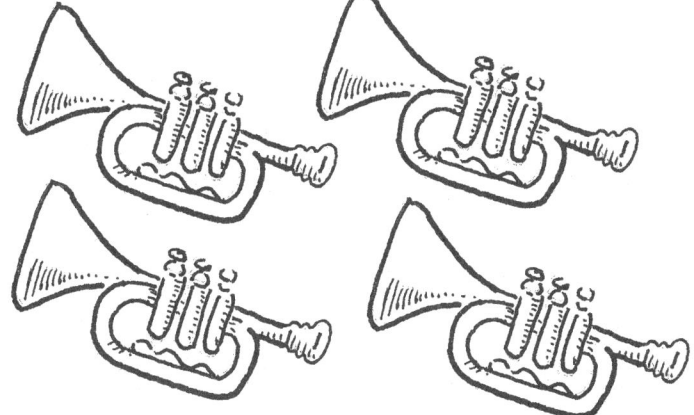

Color 4/4 of the drums.

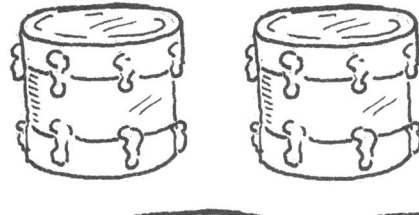
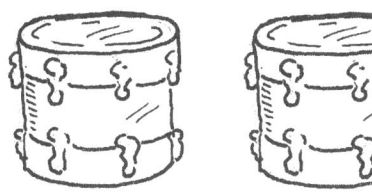

Color 0/4 of the pianos.

Name _____

Problem Solving

Story Problems

Solve these story problems.
Cut out the dinosaurs at the bottom of the page to help you.

1. Corey saw 4 dinosaurs in the forest.
   2 dinosaurs left to go swimming.
   How many dinosaurs were left? _____

2. Nicole saw 3 dinosaurs chasing butterflies.
   She also saw 1 dinosaur taking a nap.
   How many dinosaurs did she see in all? _____

3. Maya was feeding 4 dinosaurs.
   1 dinosaur could eat no more.
   How many dinosaurs were still eating? _____

Name _____

Identifying Shapes

Shape Study

A square has 4 sides.
The sides are the same size.
A square has 4 corners.
The corners are the same size.

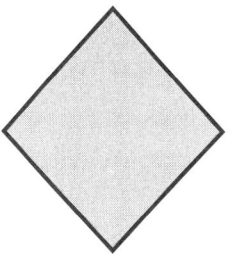

A diamond has 4 sides.
The sides are the same size.
A diamond has 4 corners.
The corners are not the same size.

A rectangle has 4 sides. Two sides
are shorter. Two sides are longer.
A rectangle has 4 corners.
The corners are the same size.

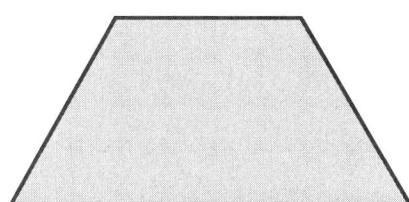

A trapezoid has 4 sides.
One side is shorter. One side
is longer. Two equal sides
connect them.

Connect the dots in the geoboards below to make shapes with 4 sides.

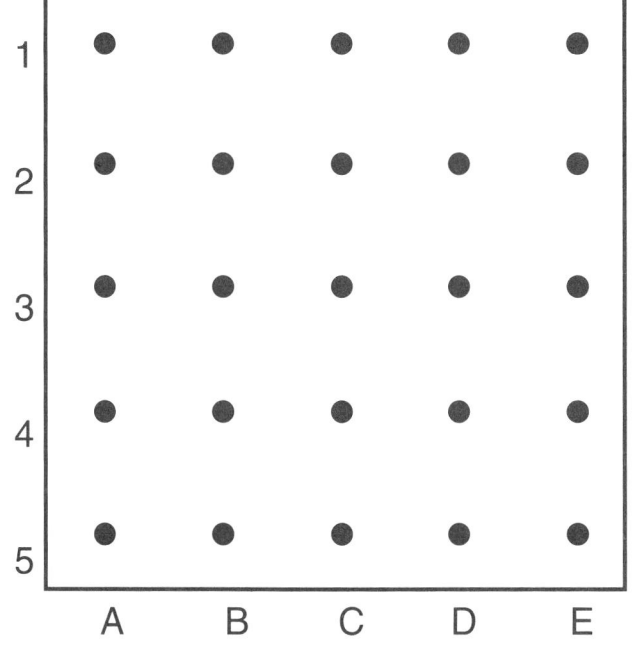
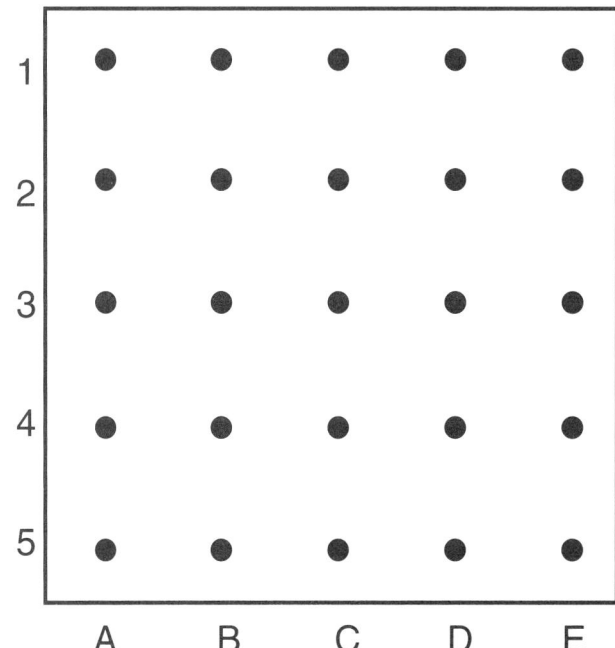

Name _____

Graphing, Counting

Graphing

A line graph has lines to show information. The graph below is a line graph. Fill it in to show 15 of your classmates' favorite subjects. First, ask each classmate which subjects they enjoy the most.

Draw a tally mark next to the subject to show the answer. Count the tallies and write the number.

music _____

art _____

math _____

P.E. _____

science _____

reading _____

writing _____

social studies _____

Follow these steps to complete the graph.

1. Find the line for the subject.
2. Find the line for its number.
3. Draw a dot where the lines meet.
4. When all the dots have been drawn, connect them. This is a line graph.
5. Which subject is most popular?

_____

Name _____

Estimating, Measuring

Measuring Length

Look at each picture. Estimate how long you think it is. Then measure each picture with a ruler. Write the actual length in inches.

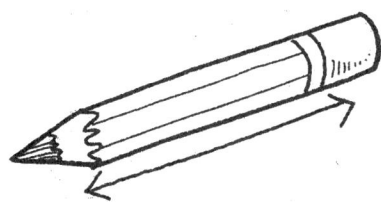

Estimate: _____ inches   Actual: _____ inches

Estimate: _____ inches   Actual: _____ inches

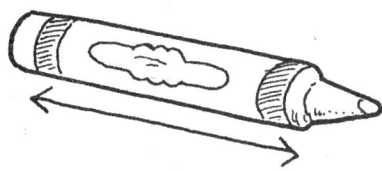

Estimate: _____ inches   Actual: _____ inches

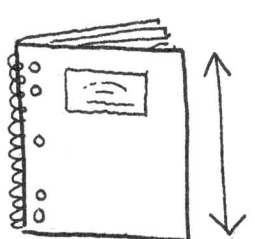

Estimate: _____ inches   Actual: _____ inches

Practice measuring other things in the room with a ruler.

Name _____   **Measuring, Fractions**

Measuring Volume

How many 1/4 cups fill 1 cup? Write your prediction: _____
Now find out. Color the correct number below.

1 cup   =   _____ 1/4 cups

• •

How many 1/4 teaspoons fill 1 tablespoon? Write your prediction: _____
Now try it. Then color the correct amount.

1 tablespoon   =   _____ 1/4 teaspoons

• •

Fill a jar with  cups of water.

Fill a jar with 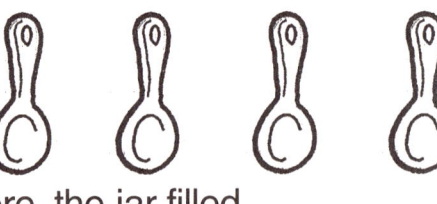 teaspoons of water.

Which jar weighs more, the jar filled
with the cups or with the teaspoons of water? _____

Explain your answer. _____

_____

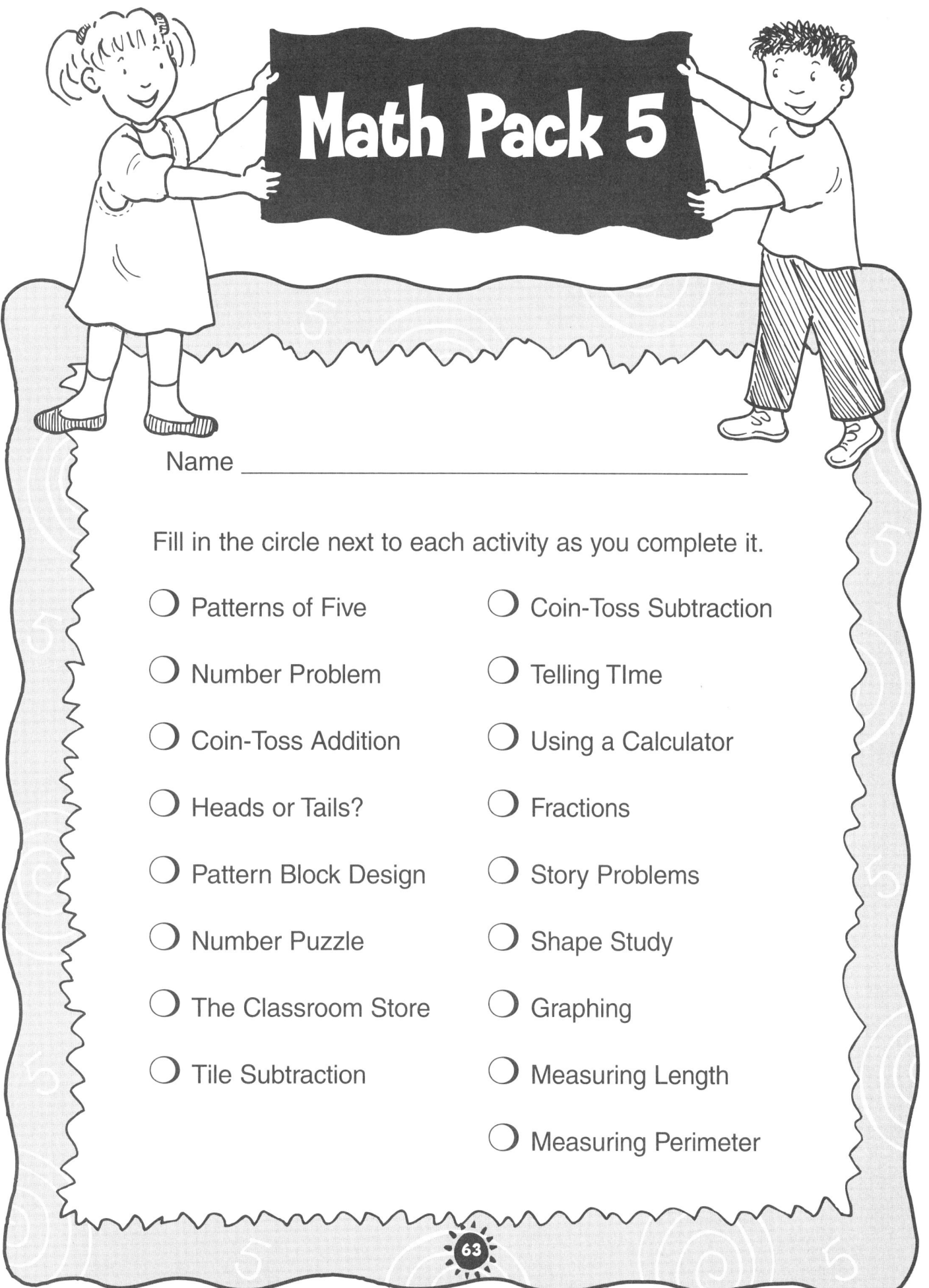

Name _____

Recognizing Patterns

Patterns of Five

Look at the number chart below. Starting with 1, count 5 squares. Color in the fifth square. Then count 5 more squares and color in the fifth square. Keep going until you reach 100.

Hundred's Chart

1	2	3	4	5	6	7	8	9	10
11	12	13	14	15	16	17	18	19	20
21	22	23	24	25	26	27	28	29	30
31	32	33	34	35	36	37	38	39	40
41	42	43	44	45	46	47	48	49	50
51	52	53	54	55	56	57	58	59	60
61	62	63	64	65	66	67	68	69	70
71	72	73	74	75	76	77	78	79	80
81	82	83	84	85	86	87	88	89	90
91	92	93	94	95	96	97	98	99	100

Tally marks can be arranged in groups of five, like this: |||| |||| ||||
Then you can count by 5's.

Count how many girls and boys are in your class.
Draw tally marks in groups of five.

Girls: _____   Boys: _____

Now count the total number. Write the totals here:

Girls: _____   Boys: _____

Name _____

Addition

Number Problem

Look at the equation below.

$3 + 2 = 5$

Make up a story to go with the equation.

Draw a picture in the box to go with your story.

Can you think of another equation that makes 5?

Write it on the line below.

Equation: _____

Coin-Toss Addition

Toss 5 coins. Write "H" for heads or "T" for tails in the circles below to show your toss. Then write the addition equation. Write the number of "heads" first. We did the first one for you. Try it three times.

Equation:  2 + 3 = 5

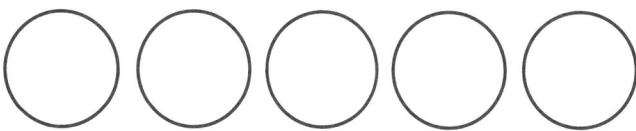

Equation: _____

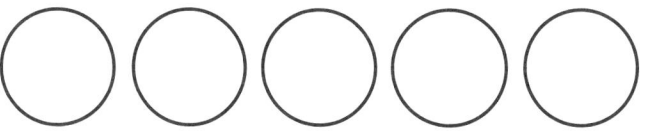

Equation: _____

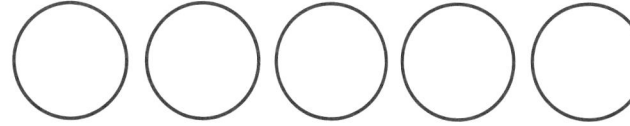

Equation: _____

Name _____

Heads or Tails?

Toss 5 pennies. Look at how the coins landed. Which equation below does it match? Color in the lowest box on the chart in the column for that equation. Toss 5 pennies again and again until one whole column has been colored. This is the combination of coins you tossed the most.

0¢ + 5¢ heads tails	1¢ + 4¢ heads tails	2¢ + 3¢ heads tails	3¢ + 2¢ heads tails	4¢ + 1¢ heads tails	5¢ + 0¢ heads tails

Probability, Addition

Name _____

Creative Thinking

Pattern Block Design

How many total pieces are in this pattern block design?

2 + 2 + 1= _____

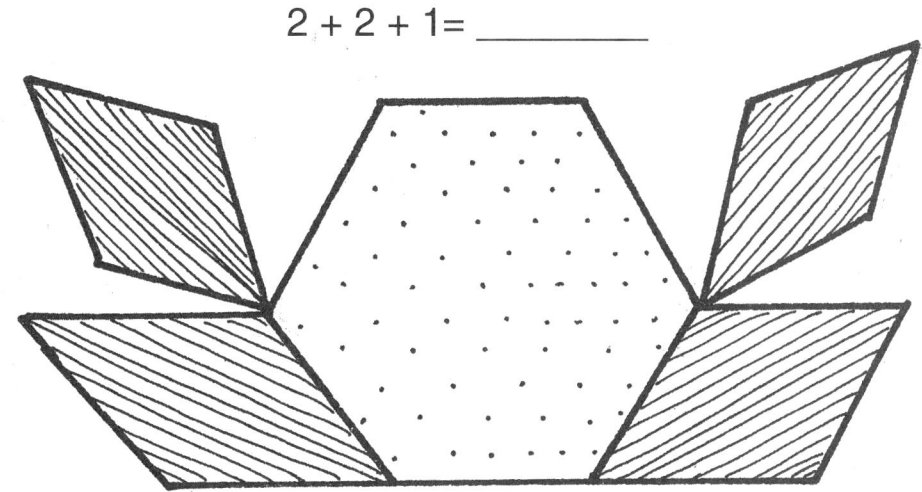

Now make your own design. Use 5 pattern blocks from the pattern block page. Cut out the shapes and trace or glue them in the space below. You may need to use a shape more than once.

Write an equation to show how many of each shape you used.

Equation: _____

Name _____

Adding, Money

Number Puzzle

These boxes form the number 5.
Write a number in each box.
You can use 0, 1, 2, 3, 4, or 5.
The sum of each row should equal 5.
The sum of each column should equal 5.

- -

The Classroom Store

Look at what is for sale in the class store. You have to spend 5¢.
You should only buy 1 thing or 2 things. Color what you will buy.

1¢   2¢   3¢   4¢   5¢

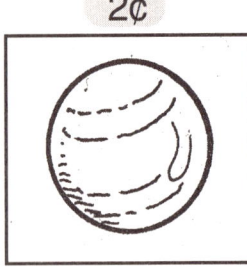   

Write an equation to show what you bought.

_____

Which coins will you give the store clerk? Color them below.

Name _____

Subtracting 5

Tile Subtraction

Take 5 tiles. Ask a classmate to hide some in his or her hand. Color in the squares below to show how many tiles are left. Write a subtraction equation to find out how many your classmate is hiding. We did the first one for you.

Equation: _5 – 3 = 2_ Equation: _____

 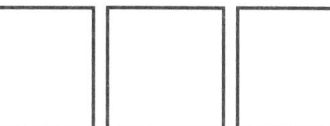

Equation: _____ Equation: _____

Coin-Toss Subtraction

Toss 5 coins. Write "H" or "T" in the circles below to show how the coins landed. ("H" = heads up; "T" = tails up.) Then finish each sentence to tell about your toss. Write a subtraction equation to show your toss, too. Write the number of heads first. For example: 5 coins - 2 heads = 3 tails

"H"=Heads   "T"=Tails

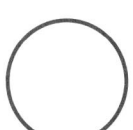    

There are _____ heads than tails.
            (more/fewer)

Subtraction equation: _____ - _____ = _____

Name _____   **Time, Calculator**

Telling Time

Draw the hands on the clock so it shows 5:00.

Draw the hands on the clock so it shows 5:30.

What do you do at 5:00? Write about it on the lines.

_____

_____

Using a Calculator

Solve the equations below. Check your answers with a calculator.

Add:

2 + 3 = _____   2 + 2 = _____

1 + 4 = _____   3 + 1 = _____

3 + 2 = _____   0 + 5 = _____

Subtract:

5 - 4 = _____   4 - 3 = _____

5 - 1 = _____   0 - 0 = _____

4 - 2 = _____   5 - 0 = _____

Name _____

Fractions, Critical Thinking

Fractions

A fraction has two numbers. The top number will tell you how many parts to color. The bottom number tells you how many parts there are.

Color 1/5 of the circle.　　　　Color 4/5 of the rectangle.

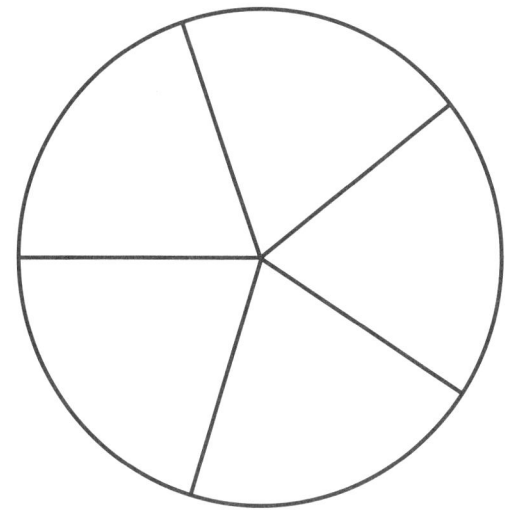
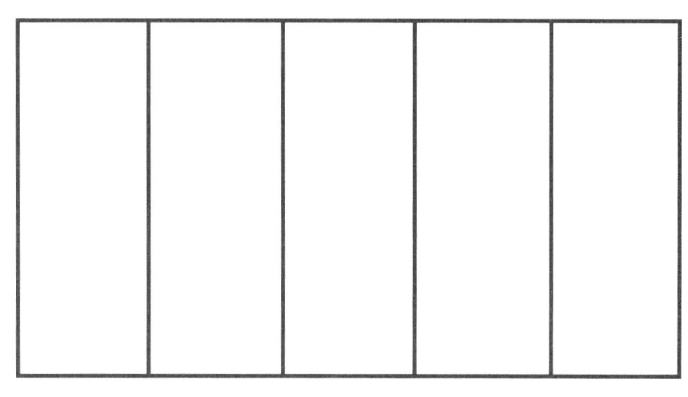

Color 3/5 of the ants.　　　　Color 2/5 of the spiders.

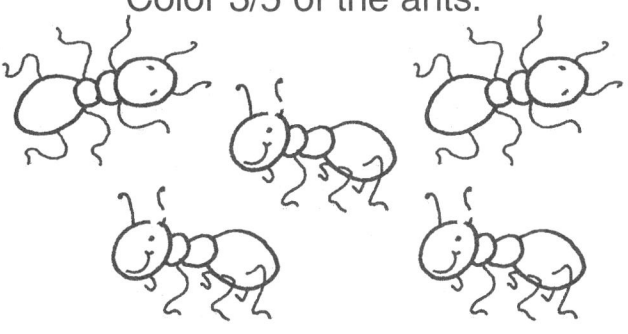
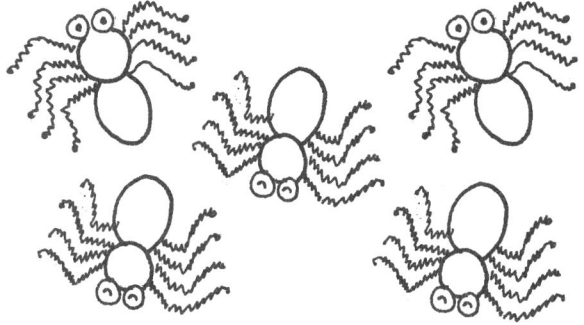

Color 0/5 of the bees.　　　　Color 5/5 of the worms.

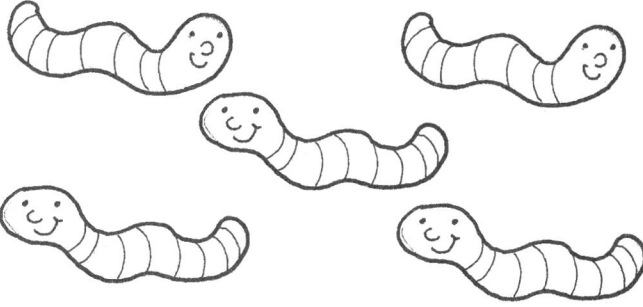

Name _____

Problem Solving

Story Problems

Solve these story problems.
Cut out the popcorn at the bottom of the page to help you.

1. Justin went to the movies.
   After he ate some, he had 5 pieces of popcorn in the cup.
   He gave 2 pieces to his friend.
   How many pieces were left? _____

2. Ethan also went to the movies.
   His dad gave him 1 piece of popcorn.
   His mom gave him 4 pieces of popcorn.
   How many pieces did Ethan eat? _____

3. Kenya went to the school carnival.
   Her friend gave her 5 pieces of popcorn.
   Kenya ate 3 pieces.
   She fed the rest to the pet goat.
   How many pieces did she give the goat? _____

Name _____

Identifying Shapes

Shape Study

A pentagon has five sides. On a pentagon, all the sides are the same length.

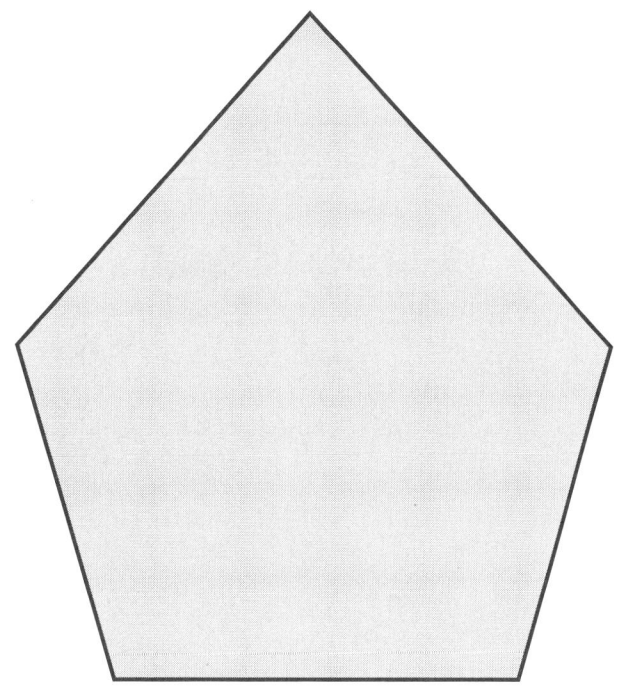

Connect the dots in the geoboards below, to make other shapes with 5 sides.

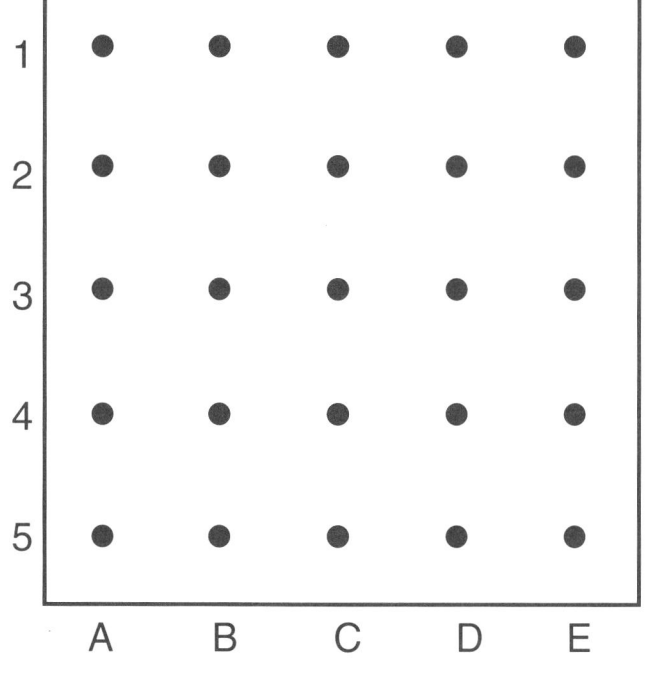
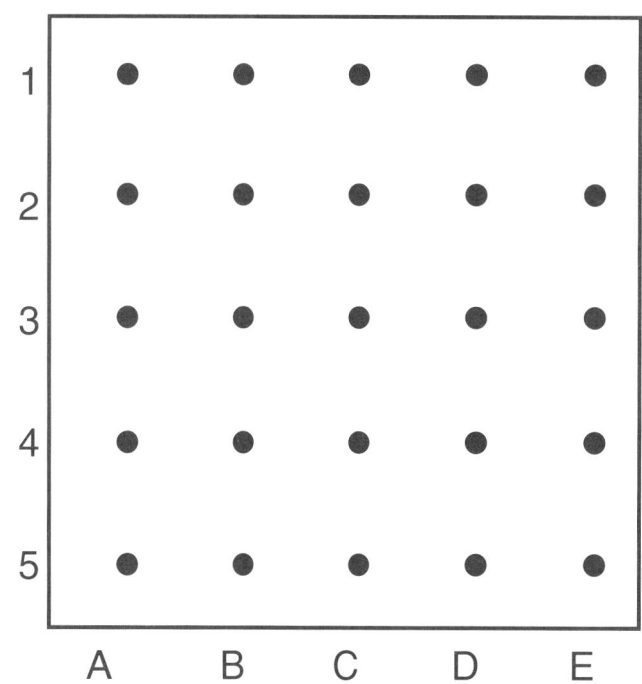

Name _____

Graphing

Graphing

We learn about the world by using our 5 senses.
The 5 senses are: seeing, hearing, smelling, touching, and tasting.

Look at the pictures on the left side of the graph. Think about which of your senses you use to learn about it. Draw a checkmark in the box to show the senses used. (Hint: You might use more than one.)

	See	Hear	Smell	Touch	Taste
rooster					
sun					
drink					
flowers					
drum					

Now graph how many senses you used for each object.

5					
4					
3					
2					
1					
	rooster	sun	drink	flowers	drum

Name _____

Measuring Length

Measuring Length

Things can be measured using inches or feet. An inch is a part of a foot. There are 12 inches in 1 foot, or: 12 inches = 1 foot.

1. Gather some small objects such as paper clips or pennies. Estimate how many of each, when lined up will equal 1 foot. Write your estimate on the chart.

2. Then line up each group of objects along a ruler that is 12 inches, or 1 foot, long. Write the actual number on the chart.

Object	Estimate	Actual

Name _____

Measuring Perimeter

Use the inch side of a ruler and measure each side of each square. Write the inches in the spaces below. Then add up all the sides to find the perimeter, or distance around each square.

____ + ____ + ____ + ____ = ____ inches

____ + ____ + ____ + ____ = ____ inches

____ + ____ + ____ + ____ = ____ inches

Math Pack 6

Name _____

Fill in the circle next to each activity as you complete it.

- ◯ Patterns of Six
- ◯ Number Problem
- ◯ Coin-Toss Addition
- ◯ Heads or Tails?
- ◯ Pattern Block Design
- ◯ Number Puzzle
- ◯ The Classroom Store
- ◯ Tile Subtraction

- ◯ Coin-Toss Subtraction
- ◯ Telling TIme
- ◯ Using a Calculator
- ◯ Fractions
- ◯ Story Problems
- ◯ Shape Study
- ◯ Graphing
- ◯ Measuring Length
- ◯ Measuring Perimeter

Name _____

Recognizing Patterns

Patterns of Six

1. A rainbow has 6 main colors: These are: red, orange, yellow, green, blue, violet.

   Color in the rainbow to show the correct order of colors.

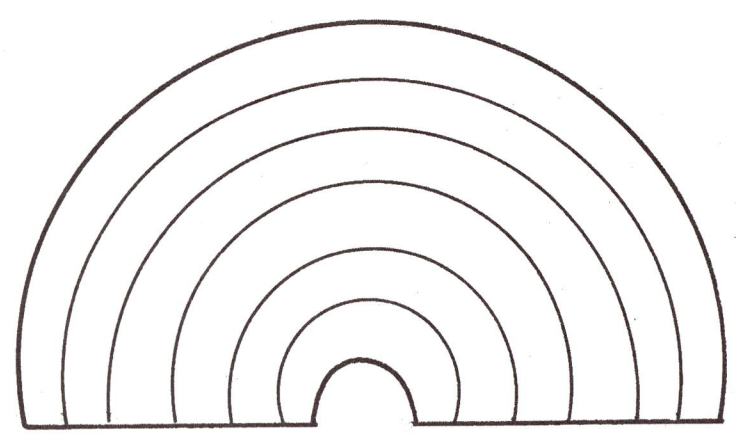

2. The colors appear in this order for a reason.
   Discover the reason by following the instructions below.

When red paint touches yellow paint, a new color forms between them.
Mix red and yellow paint to discover the new color.

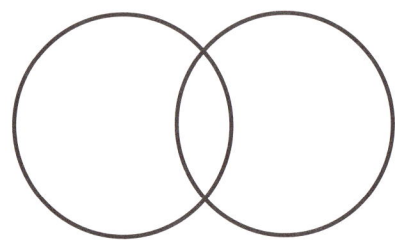   The new color is _____

When yellow paint touches blue paint, a new color forms between them.
Mix yellow and blue paint to discover the new color.

   The new color is _____

When blue paint touches red paint, a new color forms between them.
Mix blue and red paint to discover the new color.

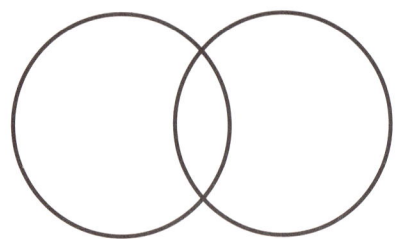   The new color is _____

Name _____

Addition

Number Problem

Look at the equation below.

3 + 3 = 6

Make up a story to go with the equation.

Draw a picture in the box to go with your story.

Now write about your picture on the lines below.

_____

_____

_____

_____

Name _____

Adding 6

Coin-Toss Addition

Toss 6 coins. Write "H" for heads or "T" for tails in the circles below to show your toss. Then write the addition equation. Write the number of "heads" first. We did the first one for you. Try it five times.

(H) (H) (H) (H) (T) (T)   Equation: 4 + 2 = 6

◯ ◯ ◯ ◯ ◯ ◯   Equation: _____

◯ ◯ ◯ ◯ ◯ ◯   Equation: _____

◯ ◯ ◯ ◯ ◯ ◯   Equation: _____

◯ ◯ ◯ ◯ ◯ ◯   Equation: _____

◯ ◯ ◯ ◯ ◯ ◯   Equation: _____

Name _____

Heads or Tails?

Toss 6 pennies. Look at how the coins landed. Which equation below does it match? Color in the lowest box on the chart in the column for that equation. Toss 6 pennies again and again until one whole column has been colored. This is the combination of coins you tossed the most.

0¢ + 6¢ heads tails	1¢ + 5¢ heads tails	2¢ + 4¢ heads tails	3¢ + 3¢ heads tails	4¢ + 2¢ heads tails	5¢ + 1¢ heads tails	6¢ + 0¢ heads tails

Probability, Adding

Pattern Block Design

How many total pieces are in this pattern block design?

2 + 2 + 1 + 1 = _____

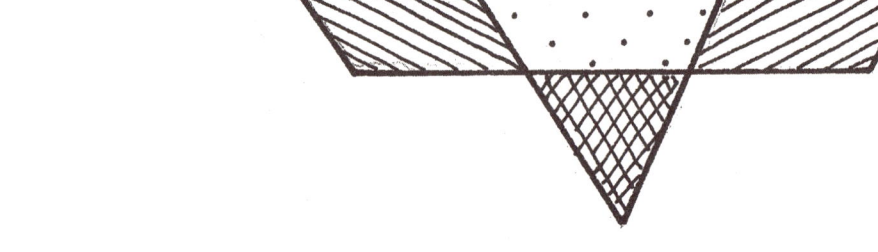

Now make your own design. Use 6 pattern blocks from the pattern block page. Cut out the shapes and trace or glue them in the space below. You may need to use a shape more than once.

Write an equation to show how many of each shape you used.

Equation: _____

Name _____

Adding

Number Puzzle

These boxes form the number 6.
Write a number in each box.
You can use 0, 1, 2, 3, 4, 5, or 6.
The sum of each row should equal 6.
The sum of each column should equal 6.

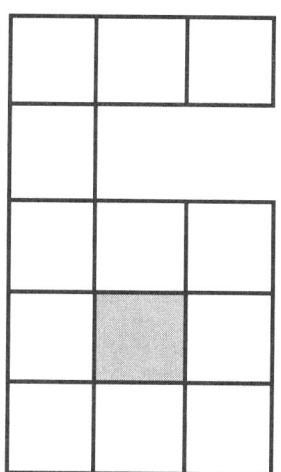

The Classroom Store

Look at what is for sale in the class store. You have to spend 6¢. You should only buy 1 thing or 2 things. Color what you will buy.

Write an equation to show what you bought.

_____

Which coins will you give the store clerk? Color them below.

Name _____

Subtracting 6

Tile Subtraction

Take 6 tiles. Ask a classmate to hide some in his or her hand. Color the squares below to show how many are left. Write a subtraction equation to find out how many tiles your classmate is hiding. We did the first one for you. Try it four times.

Equation: _____6 - 3 = 3_____

Equation: _____

Equation: _____

Equation: _____

Equation: _____

Name _____

Subtracting 6

Coin-Toss Subtraction

Toss 6 coins. Write "H" or "T" in the circles below to show how the coins landed. Then finish each sentence to tell about your toss. Write a subtraction equation to show your toss, too. Write the number of heads first. We did the first one for you. Try it two times.

"H"=Heads   "T"=Tails

There are _____more_____ heads than tails.
           (more/fewer)

Subtraction equation: ___6 coins___ - ___4 heads___ = ___2 tails___

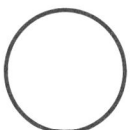     

There are _____ heads than tails.
           (more/fewer)

Subtraction equation: _____ - _____ = _____

 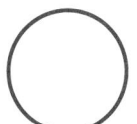   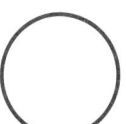 

There are _____ heads than tails.
           (more/fewer)

Subtraction equation: _____ - _____ = _____

Name _____ Time, Calculator

Telling Time

Draw the hands on the clock. so it shows 6:00.

Draw the hands on the clock. so it shows 6:30.

What do you do at 6:00 in the evening? Write about it on the lines below.

_____

_____

Using a Calculator

Solve the equations below. Check your answers with a calculator.

Add:

3 + 3 = _____   5 + 1 = _____

2 + 3 = _____   3 + 1 = _____

4 + 2 = _____   6 + 0 = _____

4 + 1 = _____   1 + 3 = _____

0 + 6 = _____   2 + 1 = _____

                        1 + 5 = _____

Subtract:

6 - 5 = _____   6 - 3 = _____

6 - 2 = _____   3 - 2 = _____

5 - 4 = _____   0 - 0 = _____

4 - 2 = _____   2 - 1 = _____

6 - 0 = _____   6 - 4 = _____

                        6 - 1 = _____

Name _____

Fractions, Critical Thinking

Fractions

A fraction has two numbers. The top number will tell you how many parts to color. The bottom number tells you how many parts there are.

Color 5/6 of the circle.   Color 3/6 of the triangle.

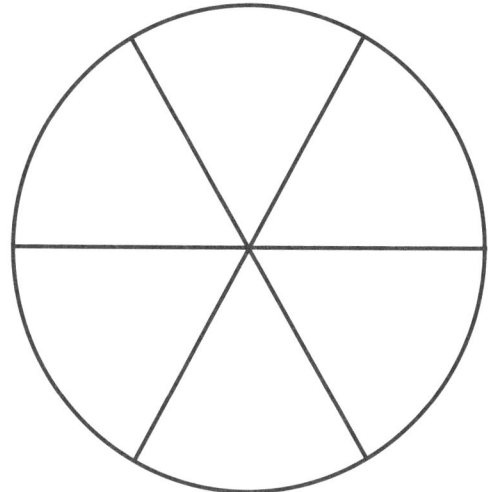
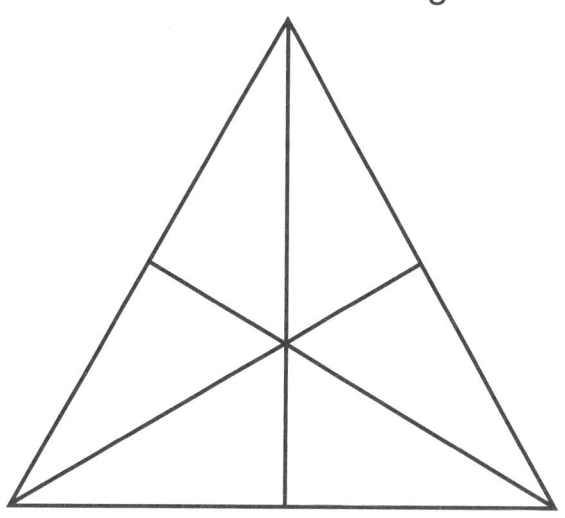

Color 6/6 of the giraffes.   Color 2/6 of the hippos.

Color 4/6 of the zebras.

Name _____

Problem Solving

Story Problems

Solve these story problems. Cut out the ice cubes at the bottom of the page to help you.

1. Brian had a glass of lemonade.
   He added 3 ice cubes.
   The lemonade still wasn't cold.
   He added 3 more cubes.
   How many did he put in the glass? _____

2. Mandy poured a glass of lemonade.
   She poured too much! The glass had 6 ice cubes.
   Mandy took out 2 cubes.
   How many were left? _____

3. Travis had a glass of lemonade.
   He added 6 ice cubes.
   5 cubes melted.
   How many were left? _____

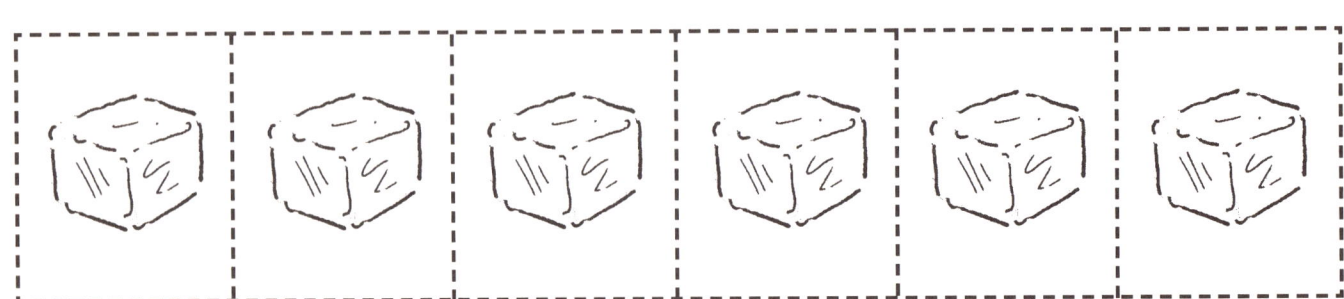

Name _____

Identifying Shapes

Shape Study

A hexagon has 6 sides. On a hexagon, all the sides are the same length.

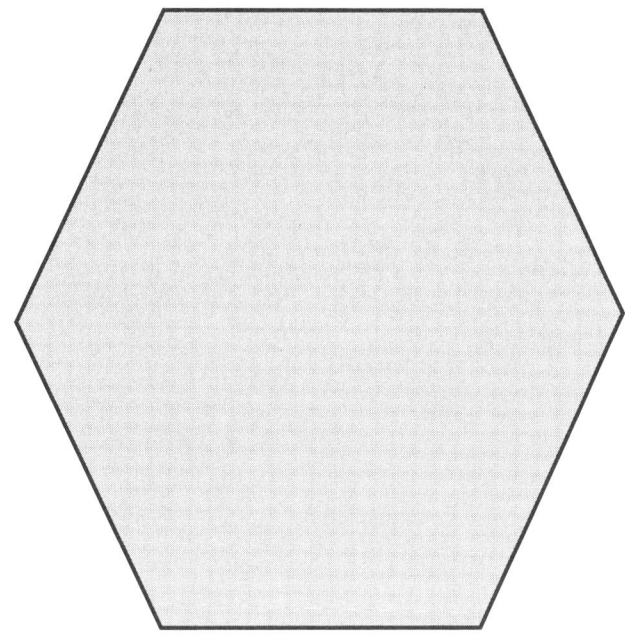

Connect the dots on the geoboards below to make other shapes with 6 sides.

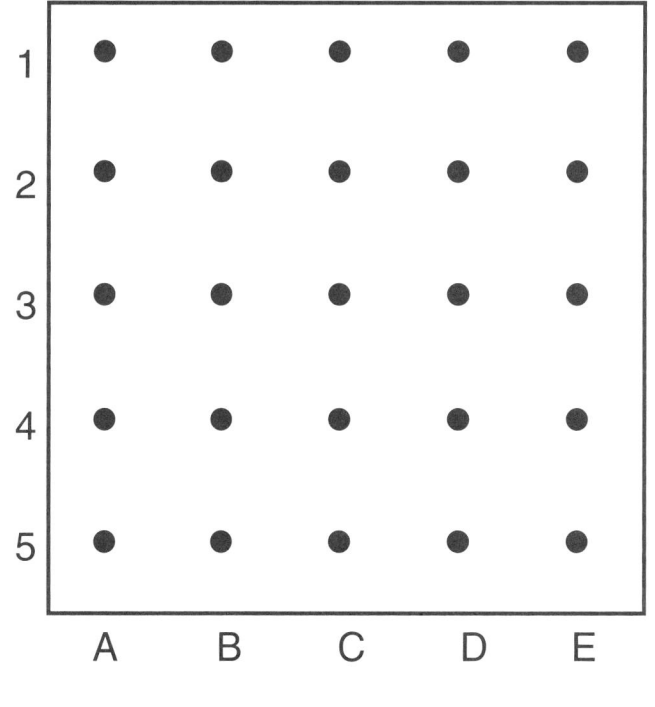
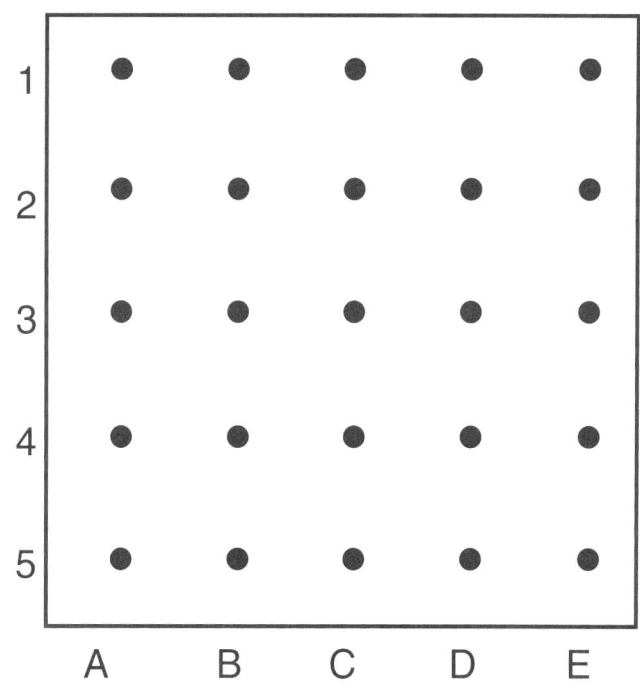

Name _____

Graphing

Graphing

Which color of the rainbow is your favorite? Color in the box for your favorite color. Have 6 classmates color the boxes to show their favorite colors, too.

Which color is liked the most? _____

Which color is liked the least? _____

Are any colors tied? _____

Which ones? _____

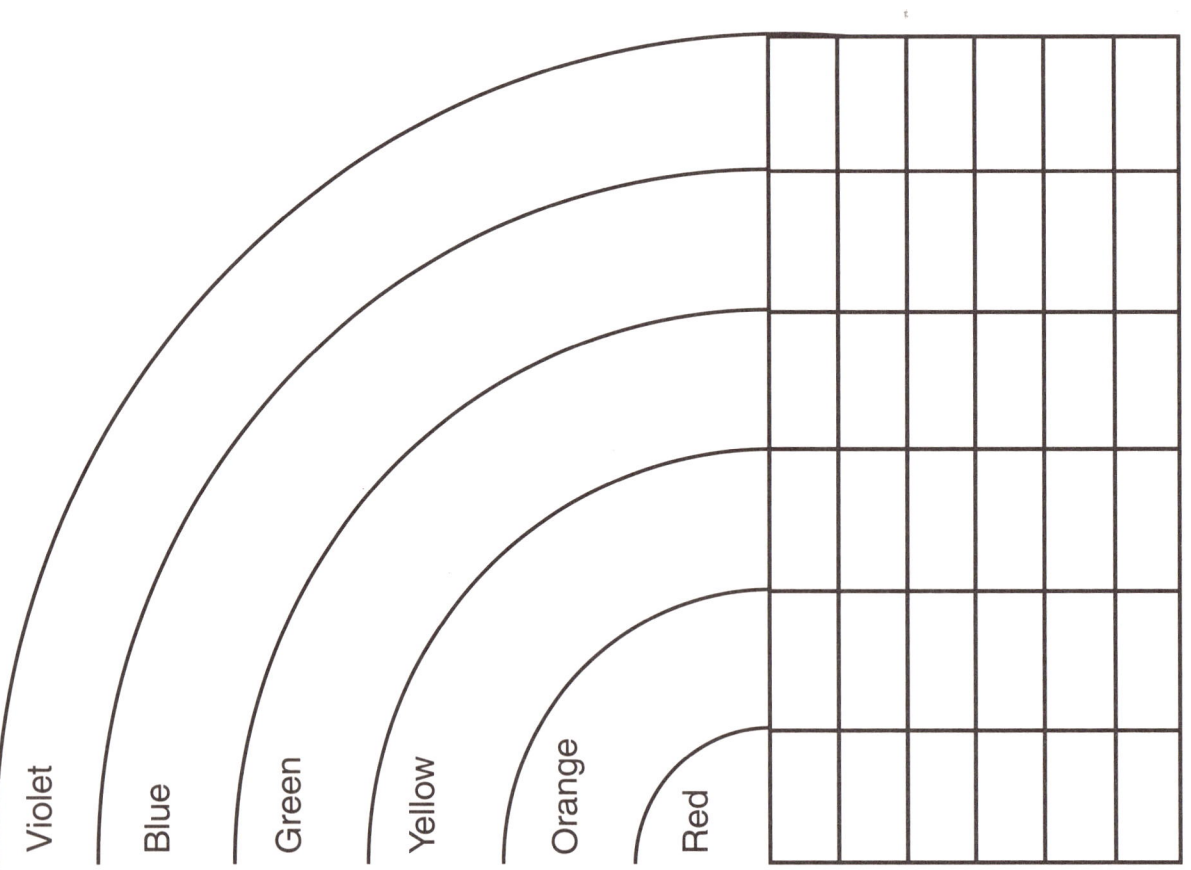

Name _____

Measuring Length

Measuring Length

Things can be measured using centimeters.
Get a ruler that measures in centimeters. Measure the pictures of the objects below.

book	book
_____ centimeters	_____ centimeters

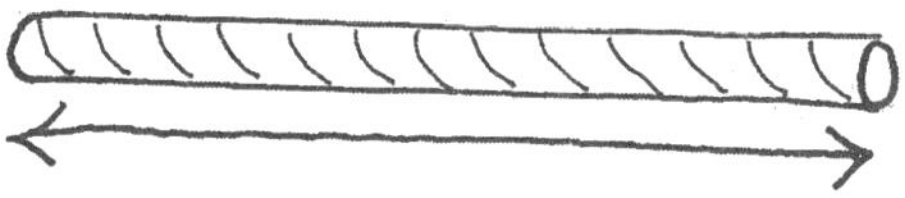

straw	marker
_____ centimeters	_____ centimeters

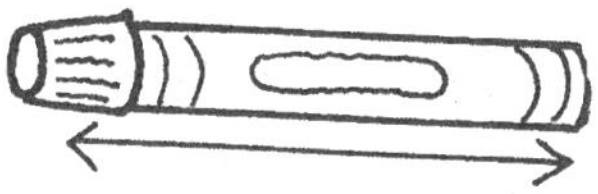

5 cubes	10 cubes
_____ centimeters	_____ centimeters

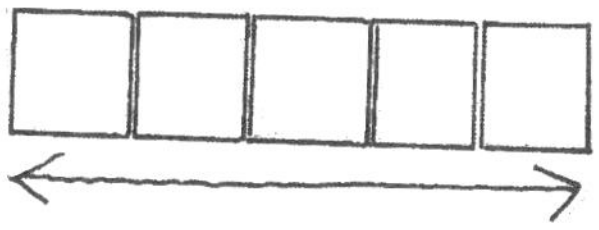

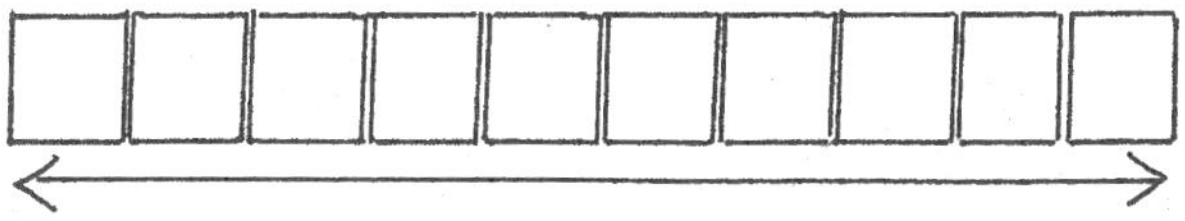

shoe	hand
_____ centimeters	_____ centimeters

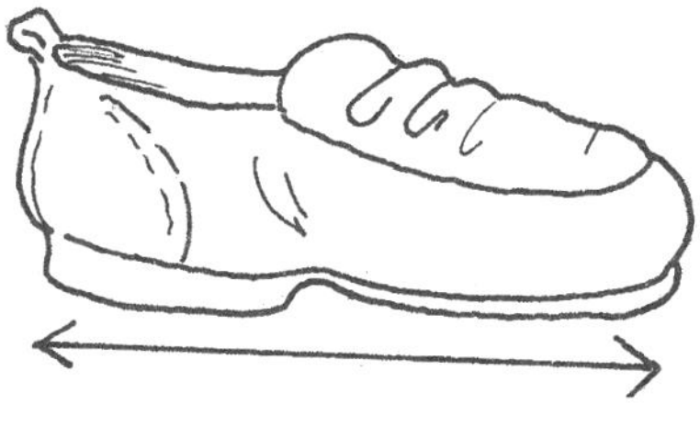

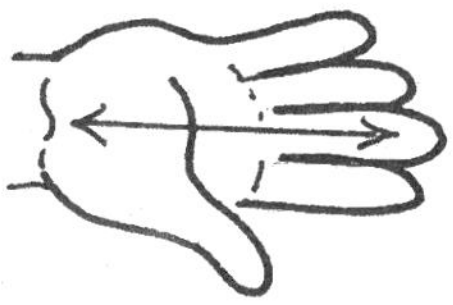

Name _____

Measuring Perimeter

Measuring Perimeter

Use the inch side of a ruler and measure each side of each rectangle. Write the inches in the spaces below. Then add up all the sides to find the perimeter, or distance, around each rectangle.

____ + ____ + ____ + ____ = ____ inches

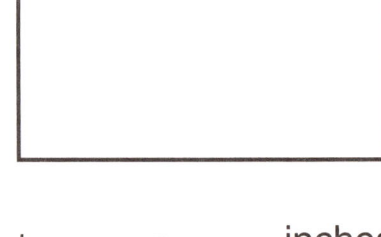

____ + ____ + ____ + ____ = ____ inches

____ + ____ + ____ + ____ = ____ inches

Math Pack 7

Name _____

Fill in the circle next to each activity as you complete it.

- ○ Patterns of Seven
- ○ Number Problem
- ○ Coin-Toss Addition
- ○ Heads or Tails?
- ○ Pattern Block Design
- ○ Number Puzzle
- ○ The Classroom Store
- ○ Tile Subtraction

- ○ Coin-Toss Subtraction
- ○ Telling Time
- ○ Using a Calculator
- ○ Fractions
- ○ Story Problems
- ○ Shape Study
- ○ Graphing
- ○ Measuring Length
- ○ Measuring Perimeter

Name _____

Recognizing Patterns

Patterns of Seven

1. The days of the week are a pattern of 7. Every week, the days repeat in the same way. Look at the calendar below. Read the days of the week across the top. Say them out loud.

JANUARY						
Sunday	Monday	Tuesday	Wednesday	Thursday	Friday	Saturday
			1	2	3	
4	5	6	7	8	9	10
11	12	13	14	15	16	17
18	19	20	21	22	23	24
25	26	27	28	29	30	31

Answer these questions about the calendar above.

1. Which month is it? _____

2. How many days are in this month? _____

3. How many days are in one full week? _____

4. How many days are in two full weeks? _____

5. On what day of the week is January 1? _____

6. What is the date 1 week later? _____

7. How many Wednesdays are there? _____

8. What is the date of the last Friday? _____

With a classmate, talk about the different patterns you see.

Name _____

Addition

Number Problem

Look at the equation below.

4 + 3 = 7

Make up a story to go with the equation.

Draw a picture in the box to go with your story.

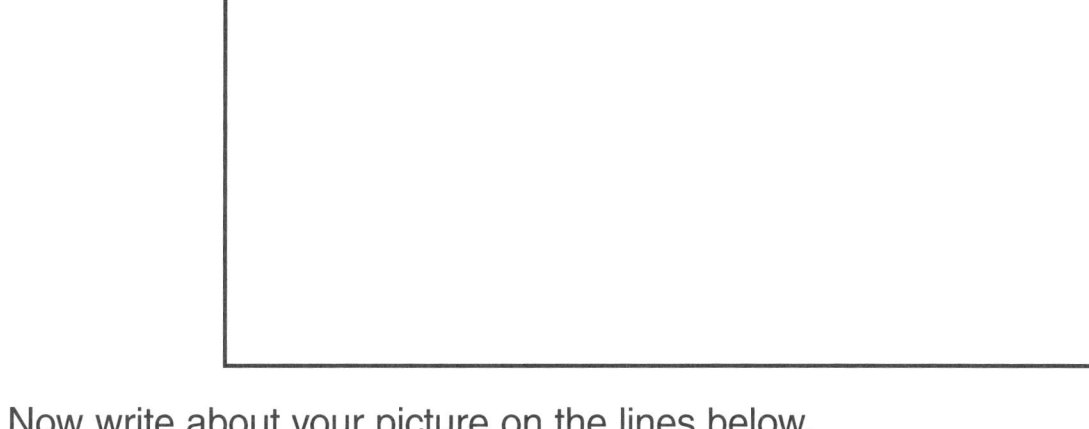

Now write about your picture on the lines below.

_____

_____

_____

_____

_____

Name _____

Adding 7

Coin-Toss Addition

Toss 7 coins. Write "H" for heads or "T" for tails in the circles below to show your toss. Then write the addition equation. Write the number of "heads" first. We did the first one for you. Try it three times.

Equation: 3 + 4 = 7

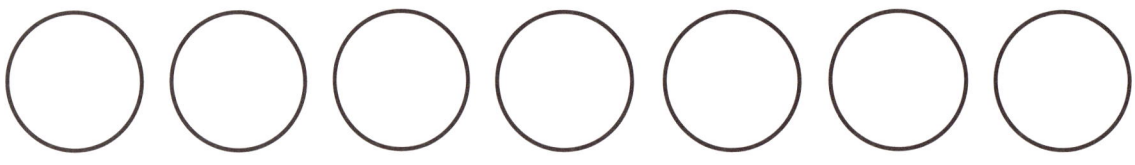

Equation: _____

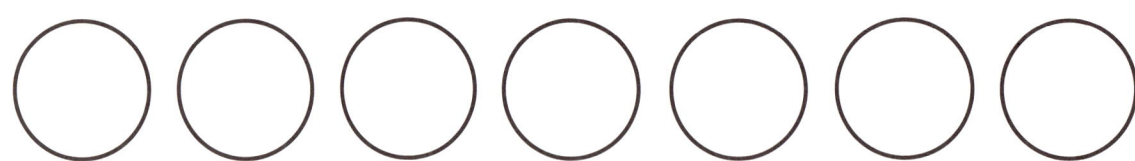

Equation: _____

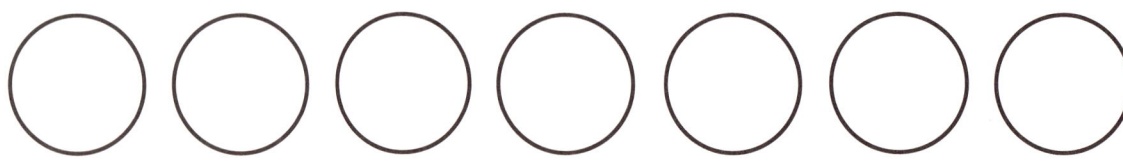

Equation: _____

Name _____

Heads or Tails?

Toss 7 pennies. Look at how the coins landed. Which equation below does it match? Color in the lowest box on the chart in the column for that equation. Toss 7 pennies again and again until one whole column has been colored. This is the combination of coins you tossed the most.

| 0¢ + 7¢ | 1¢ + 6¢ | 2¢ + 5¢ | 3¢ + 4¢ | 4¢ + 3¢ | 5¢ + 2¢ | 6¢ + 1¢ | 7¢ + 0¢ |
| heads tails | heads tails | heads tails | heads tails | heads tails | heads tails | heads tails | heads tails |

Probability, Adding

7

Name _____

Creative Thinking

Pattern Block Design

How many total pieces are in this pattern block design?

1 + 2 + 4 = _____

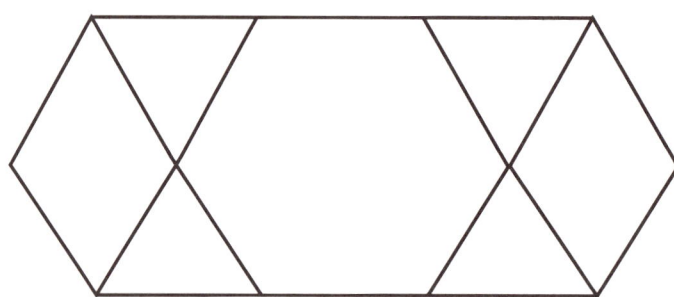

Now make your own design. Use 7 pattern blocks from the pattern block page. Cut out the shapes and trace or glue them in the space below. You may need to use a shape more than once.

Write an equation to show how many of each shape you used.

Equation: _____

Name _____

Adding, Money

Number Puzzle

These boxes form the number 7.
Write a number in each box.
You can use 0, 1, 2, 3, 4, 5, 6, or 7
The sum of the row should equal 7.
The sum of the column should equal 7.

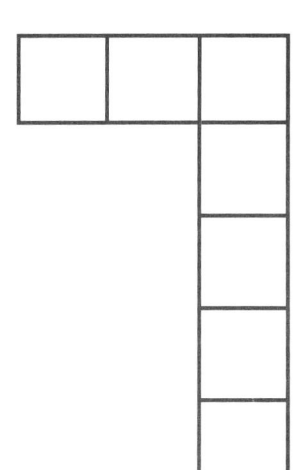

The Classroom Store

Look at what is for sale in the classroom store. You have to spend 7¢.
You should only buy 1 thing, 2 things, or 3 things. Color what you will buy.

Write an equation to show you what you bought.

_____

Which coins will you give the store clerk? Color them below.

Name _____   **Subtracting 7**

Tile Subtraction

Take 7 tiles. Ask a classmate to hide some in his or her hand. Color the squares below to show how many tiles are left. Write a subtraction equation to find out how many tiles your classmate is hiding. We did the first one for you. Try it four times.

Equation: _____ 7 - 2 = 5 _____

Equation: _____

Equation: _____

Equation: _____

Equation: _____

Name _____

Subtracting 7

Coin-Toss Subtraction

Toss 7 coins. Write "H" for heads or "T" for tails in the circles below to show how the coins landed. Then finish each sentence to tell about your toss. Write a subtraction equation to show your toss, too. Write the number of heads first. We did the first one for you. Try it two times.

"H"=Heads   "T"=Tails

There are ____fewer____ heads than tails.
(more/fewer)

Subtraction equation: __7 coins__ - __3 heads__ = __4 tails__

  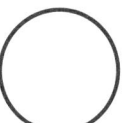   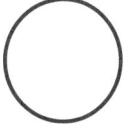 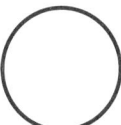

There are _____ heads than tails.
(more/fewer)

Subtraction equation: _____ - _____ = _____

  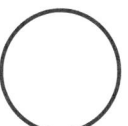 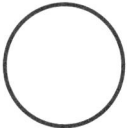  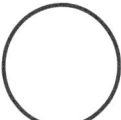 

There are _____ heads than tails.
(more/fewer)

Subtraction equation: _____ - _____ = _____

Name _____

Time

Telling Time

Draw hands on the clock so it shows 7:00.

Draw hands on the clock so it shows 7:30.

What do you do at 7:00 in the evening?

_____

What do you do at 7:00 in the morning?

_____

Using a Calculator

Solve the equations below. Check your answers with a calculator.

Add:

5 + 2 = _____
6 + 0 = _____
3 + 4 = _____
2 + 4 = _____
3 + 2 = _____

1 + 6 = _____
0 + 7 = _____
3 + 3 = _____
2 + 5 = _____
1 + 4 = _____

Subtract:

7 - 6 = _____
7 - 4 = _____
5 - 4 = _____
7 - 0 = _____
4 - 3 = _____

1 - 1 = _____
7 - 5 = _____
7 - 3 = _____
6 - 4 = _____
7 - 2 = _____

Name _____

Fractions, Critical Thinking

Fractions

A fraction has two numbers. The top number will tell you how many parts to color. The bottom number tells you how many total parts there are.

Color 1/7 of the candy.   Color 4/7 of the candy.

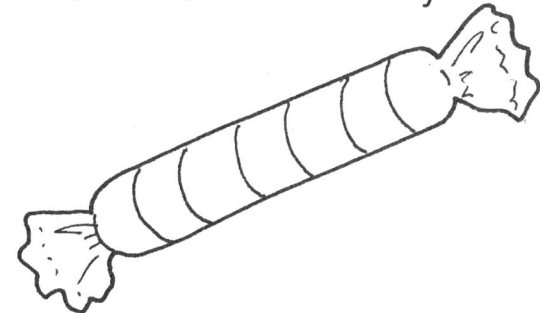 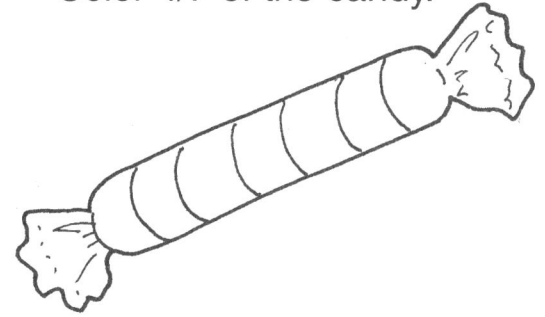

This loaf of bread is cut into 7 slices.

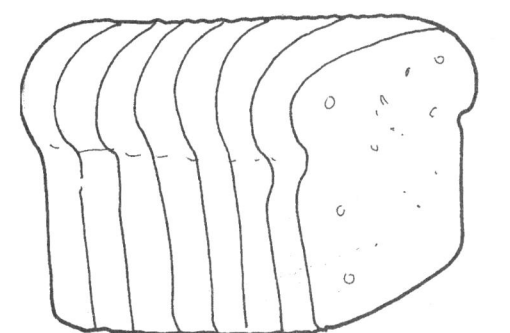

Could you color 8/7 of the bread? _____

Explain your answer. _____

Color 7/7 of the bananas.   Color 3/7 of the peanut butter jars.

Name _____

Problem Solving

Story Problems

Solve these story problems.
Cut out the flowers at the bottom of the page to help you.

1. Jared had a flowerpot with 7 flowers.
   He replanted 5 flowers outdoors.
   How many flowers were left in the pot? _____

2. Kristin planted 7 flowers.
   1 flower wilted.
   How many flowers were not wilted? _____

3. Hannah picked flowers for her father.
   She picked 3 flowers from the front yard.
   She picked 4 flowers from the back yard.
   She put them in a flowerpot.
   How many flowers did Hannah pick? _____

Name _____

Identifying Shapes

Shape Study

A heptagon has 7 sides. On a heptagon, all the sides are the same length.

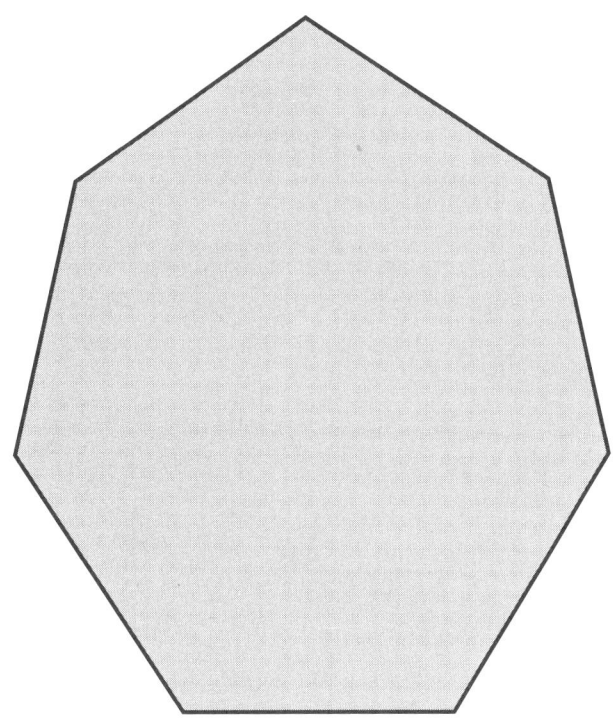

Connect the dots in the geoboards below to make other shapes with 7 sides.

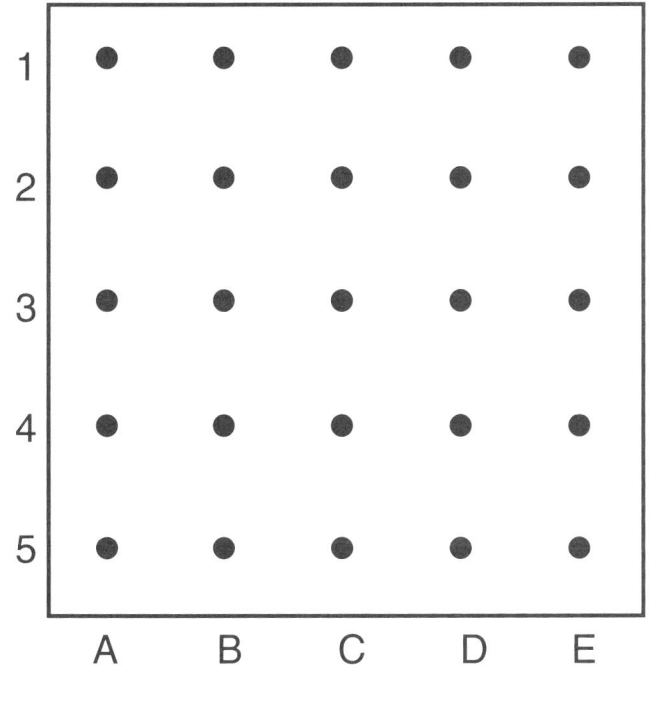
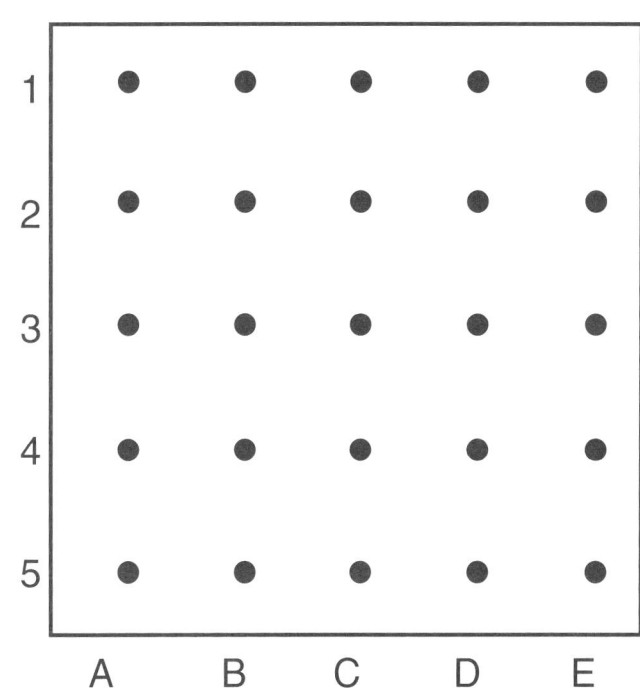

Name _____

Graphing

Graphing

The picture was made with 7 different shapes. How many of each shape was used? Color in the shapes, following the instructions. Then color in the boxes on the chart, 1 box for each shape used.

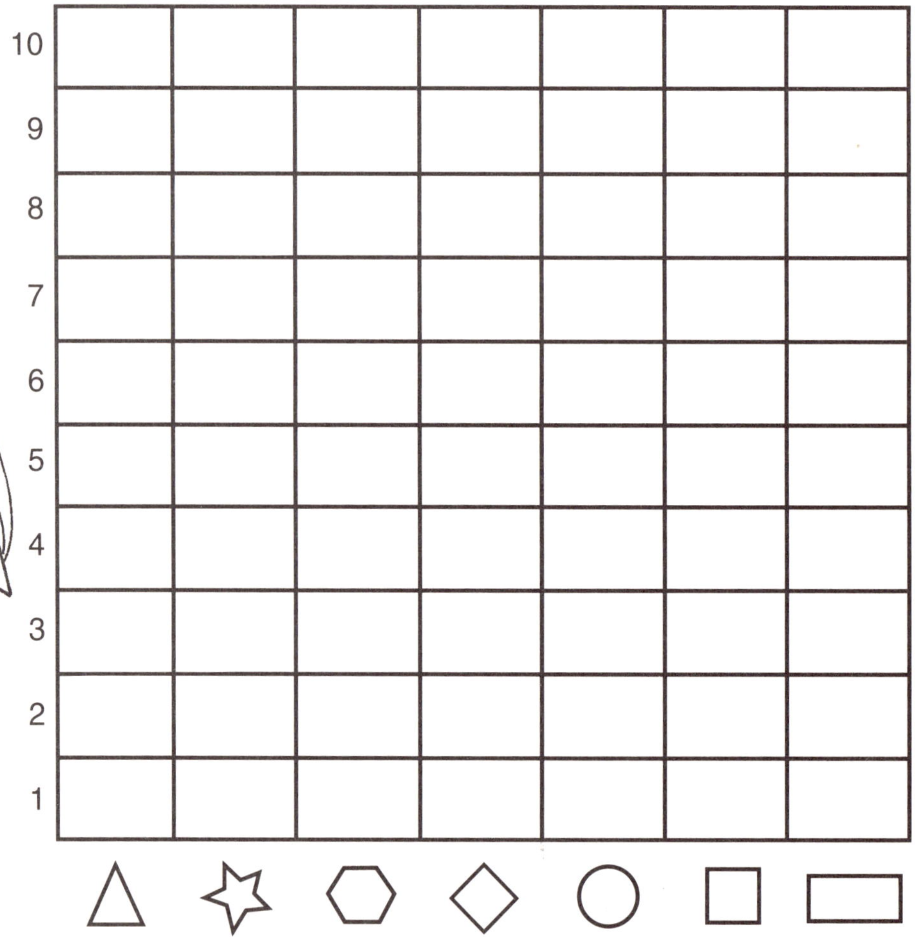

Color the  △ red. Color the ⬡ green. Color the ○ blue.
Color the ☆ black. Color the ◇ orange. Color the ▢ yellow.
                                          Color the ▭ purple.

Which shape was used the most? _____

Name _____

Measuring Length

Measuring Length

Look at the curvy lines.
Estimate how many inches each is.
Lay a piece of string along each line.
Measure the strings to find out how many inches the curvy lines really are.

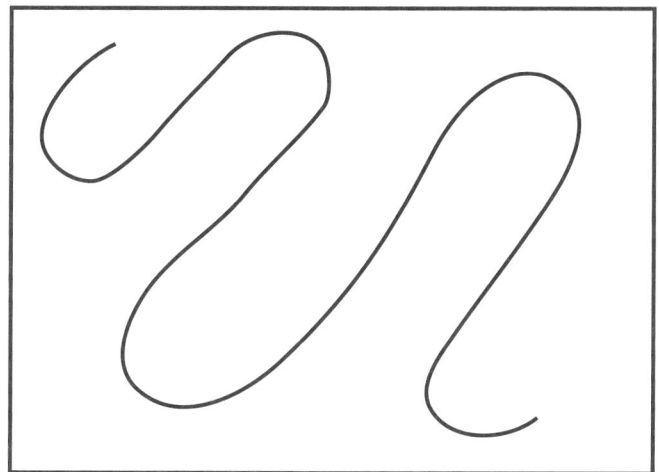

Estimate: _____

Actual: _____

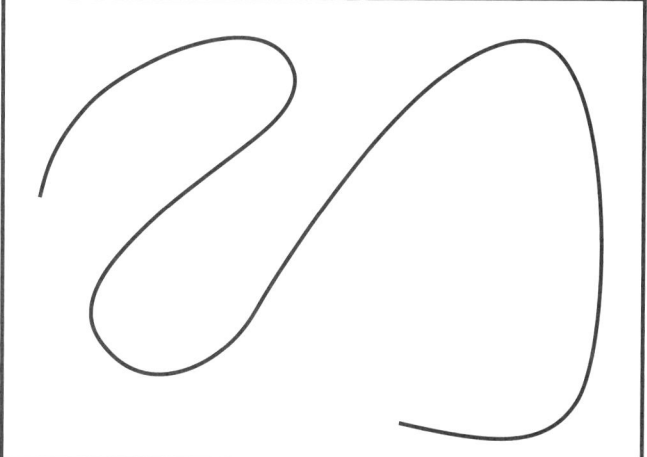

Estimate: _____

Actual: _____

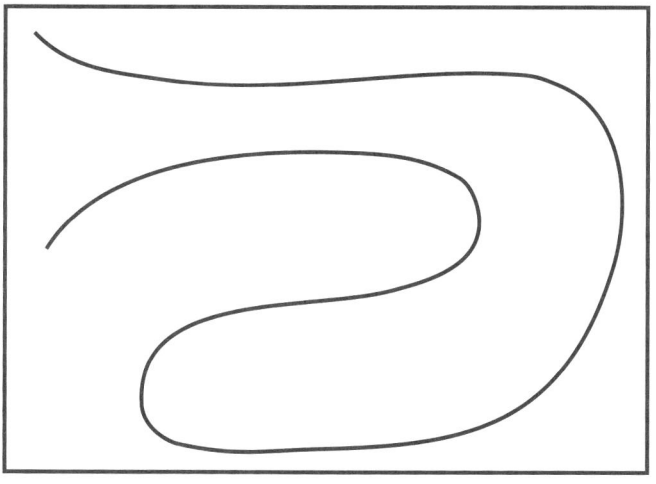

Estimate: _____

Actual: _____

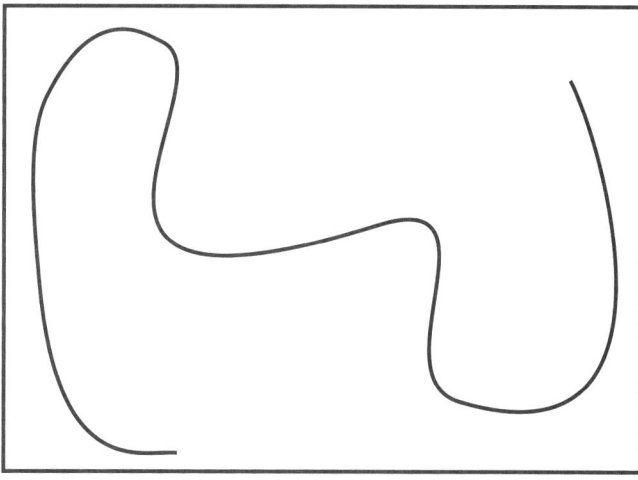

Estimate: _____

Actual: _____

Name _____

Measuring Perimeter

Measuring Perimeter

Use the inch side of a ruler and measure each side of each triangle. Write the inches in the spaces below. Then add up all the sides to find the perimeter, or distance around each triangle.

____ + ____ + ____ = ____ inches

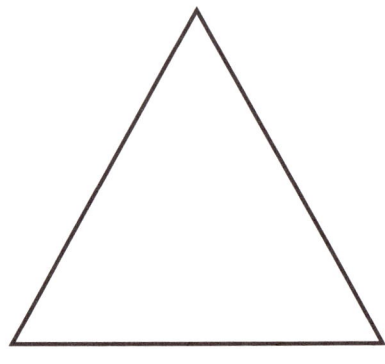

____ + ____ + ____ = ____ inches

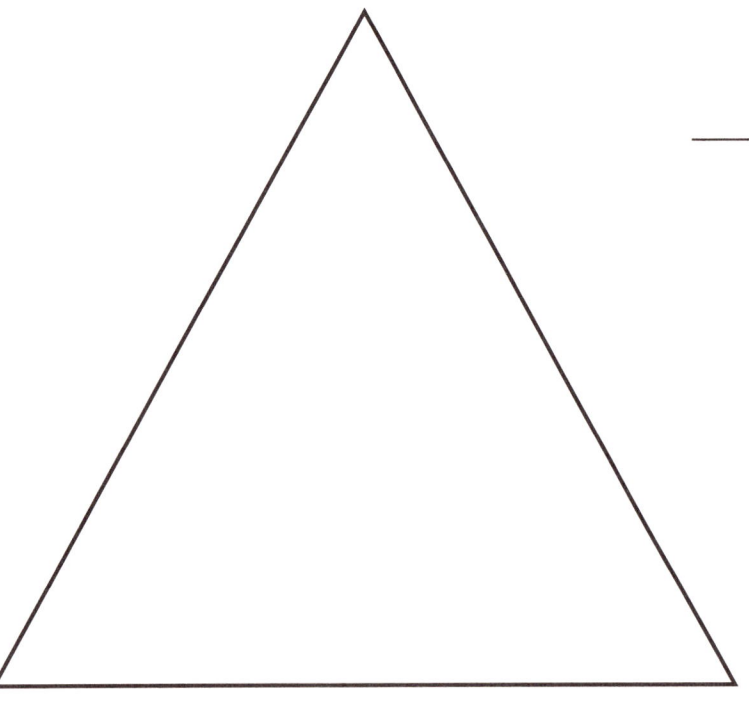

____ + ____ + ____ = ____ inches

Math Pack 8

Name _____

Fill in the circle next to each activity you complete.

- ○ Patterns of Eight
- ○ Number Problem
- ○ Coin-Toss Addition
- ○ Heads or Tails?
- ○ Pattern Block Design
- ○ Number Puzzle
- ○ The Classroom Store
- ○ Tile Subtraction

- ○ Coin-Toss Subtraction
- ○ Telling Time
- ○ Using a Calculator
- ○ Fractions
- ○ Story Problems
- ○ Shape Study
- ○ Graphing
- ○ Measuring Length
- ○ Measuring Volume

Name _____

Recognizing Patterns

Patterns of Eight

1. Draw an animal with 8 legs. It can be real or pretend.

2. Crayons sometimes come in boxes with 8 colors. Look at the crayon box below.

Which 2 colors in this box are not in the rainbow?

_____

_____

What is your favorite color? _____

Ask 8 friends if they like that color, too.

Draw tally marks to show the number of friends who like the same color as you: _____

Name _____

Addition

Number Problem

Look at the equation below.

4 + 4 = 8

Make up a story to go with the equation.

Draw a picture in the box to go with your story.

Now write about your picture on the lines below.

_____

_____

_____

_____

_____

Name _____

Adding 8

Coin-Toss Addition

Toss 8 coins. Write "H" for heads or "T" for tails in the circles below to show your toss. Then write the addition equation. Write the number of "heads" first. We did the first one for you. Try it three times.

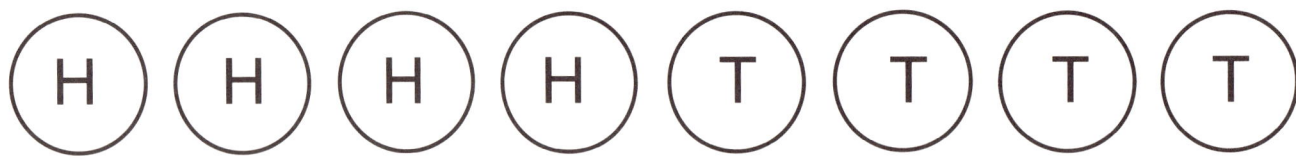

Equation: _____ 4 + 4 = 8 _____

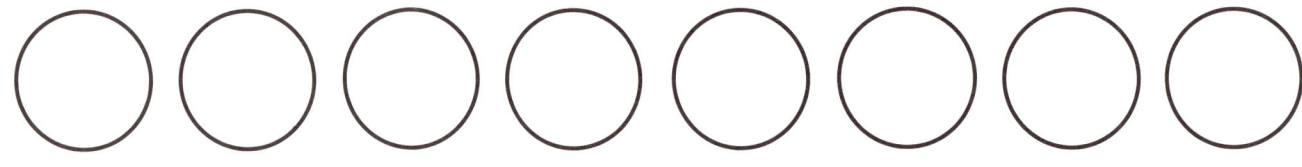

Equation: _____

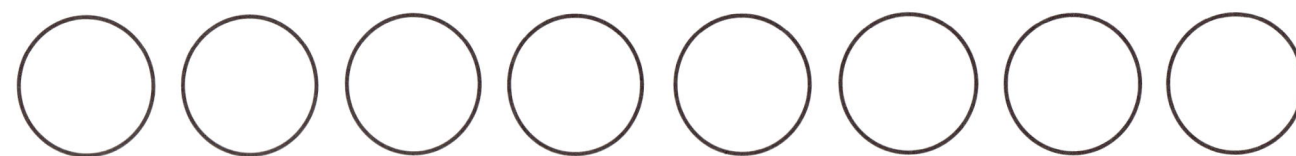

Equation: _____

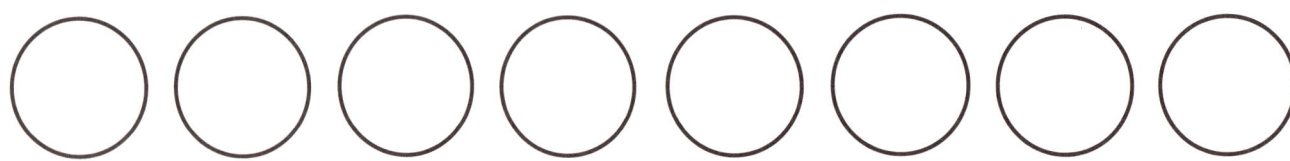

Equation: _____

Name _____

Heads or Tails?

Toss 8 pennies. Look at how the coins landed. Which equation below does it match? Color in the lowest box on the chart in the column for that equation. Toss 8 pennies again and again until one whole column has been colored. This is the combination of coins you tossed the most.

Probability, Adding

| 0¢ + 8¢ | 1¢ + 7¢ | 2¢ + 6¢ | 3¢ + 5¢ | 4¢ + 4¢ | 5¢ + 3¢ | 6¢ + 2¢ | 7¢ + 1¢ | 8¢ + 0¢ |
| heads tails | heads tails | heads tails | heads tails | heads tails | heads tails | heads tails | heads tails | heads tails |

Name _____

Creative Thinking

Pattern Block Design

How many total pieces are in this pattern block design?

3 + 5 = _____

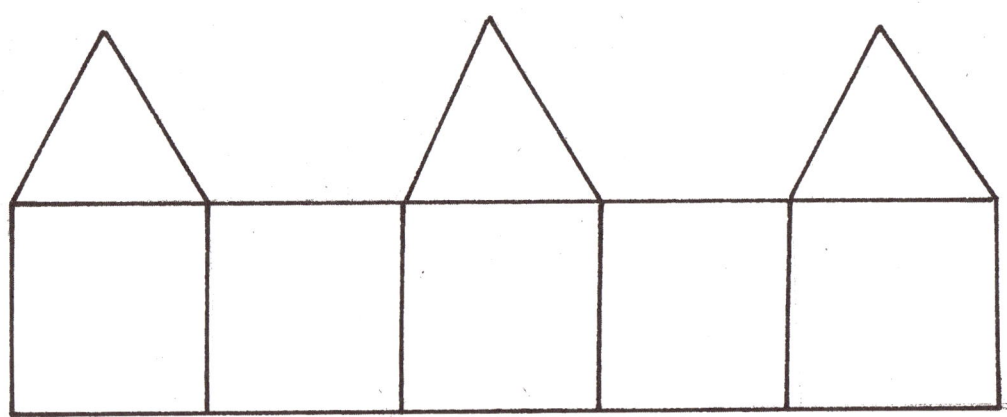

Now make your own design. Use 8 pattern blocks from the pattern block page. Cut out the shapes and trace or glue them in the space below. You may need to use a shape more than once.

Write an equation to show how many of each shape you used.

Equation: _____

Name _____

Adding, Money

Number Puzzle

These boxes form the number 8.
Write a number in each box.
You can use 0, 1 ,2, 3, 4, 5, 6, 7, or 8.
The sum of each row should equal 8.
The sum of each column should equal 8.

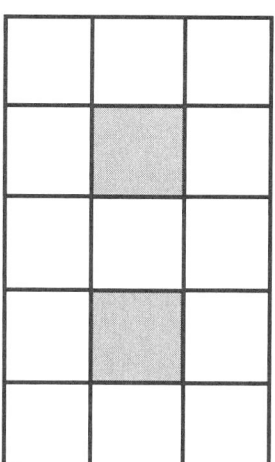

The Classroom Store

Look at what is for sale in the class store. You have to spend 8¢. You should buy only 1 thing, 2 things, or 3 things. Color what you will buy.

Write an equation to show what you bought.

_____

Which coins will you give the store clerk? Color them below.

Name _____

Subtracting 8

Tile Subtraction

Take 8 tiles. Ask a classmate to hide some in his or her hand. Color the squares below to show how many tiles are left. Write the subtraction equation to find out how many tiles your classmate is hiding. We did the first one for you. Try it four times.

Equation: ___8 - 4 = 4___

Equation: _____

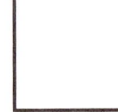

Equation: _____

Equation: _____

Equation: _____

Name _____

Subtracting 8

Coin-Toss Subtraction

Toss 8 coins. Write "H" for heads or "T" for tails in the circles below to show how the coins landed. Then finish each sentence to tell about your toss. Write a subtraction equation to show your toss, too. Write the number of heads first. We did the first one for you. Try it two times.

"H"=Heads   "T"=Tails

There are _____more_____ heads than tails.
(more/fewer)

Subtraction equation: __8 coins__ - __5 heads__ = __3 tails__

There are _____ heads than tails.
(more/fewer)

Subtraction equation: _____ - _____ = _____

There are _____ heads than tails.
(more/fewer)

Subtraction equation: _____ - _____ = _____

Name _____   Time, Calculator

Telling Time

Draw the hands on the clock so it shows 8:00.

Draw the hands on the clock so it shows 8:30.

If it's 8:00, what time was it an hour ago?
_____

If it's 8:30, what time was it an hour ago?
_____

Using a Calculator

Solve the equations below. Check your answers with a calculator.

Add: **Subtract:**

3 + 5 = ____   2 + 6 = ____   8 + 0 = ____   8 - 7 = ____   8 - 3 = ____   8 - 4 = ____

2 + 5 = ____   5 + 3 = ____   1 + 6 = ____   4 - 3 = ____   8 - 0 = ____   8 - 2 = ____

4 + 4 = ____   0 + 8 = ____   6 + 2 = ____   8 - 5 = ____   6 - 5 = ____   7 - 5 = ____

1 + 7 = ____   7 + 1 = ____   2 + 5 = ____   6 - 4 = ____   3 - 1 = ____   1 - 0 = ____

3 + 4 = ____   4 + 3 = ____   1 + 3 = ____   8 - 8 = ____   8 - 6 = ____   8 - 1 = ____

Name _____

Fractions, Critical Thinking

Fractions

A fraction has two numbers. The top number will tell you how many parts to color. The bottom number tells you how many parts there are.

Color 1/8 of the circle.

Color 6/8 of the square.

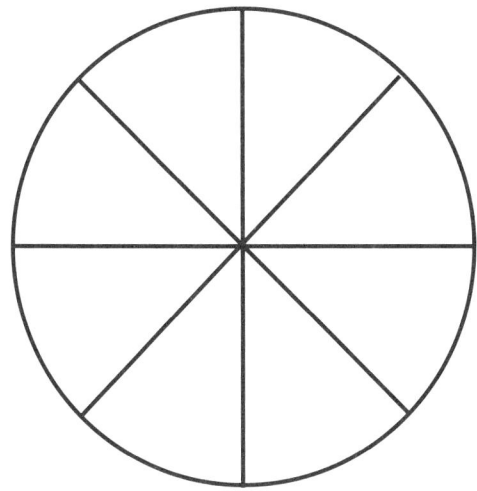
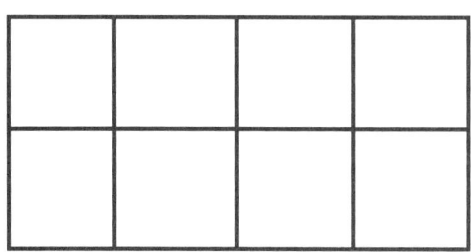

Color 4/8 of the suns.

Color 8/8 of the stars.

Color 2/8 of the moons.

Color 3/8 of the planets.

Name _____

Problem Solving

Story Problems

Solve these story problems.
Cut out the crayons at the bottom of the page to help you.

1. Alex had 8 crayons.
   He lost 2 during art class.
   How many crayons did he have left? _____

2. Cassie has 4 neon crayons.
   She has 4 glitter crayons, too.
   How many crayons does Cassie have in all? _____

3. Clayton took 8 crayons outside.
   The dog ran off with 1 crayon.
   The sun melted 2 more crayons.
   How many crayons did Clayton have left? _____

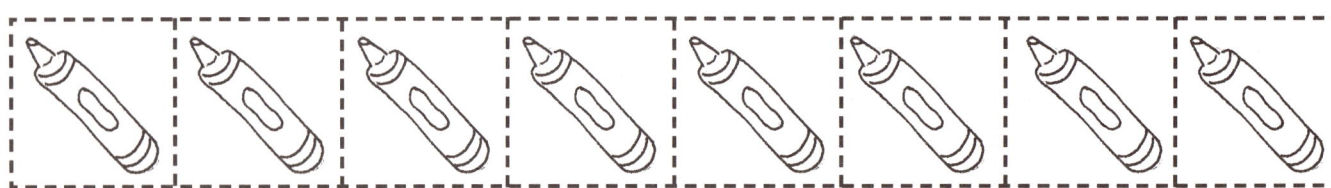

Name _____

Identifying Shapes

Shape Study

An octagon has 8 sides. On an octagon, all the sides are the same length.

Connect the dots in the geoboards below to make other shapes with 8 sides.

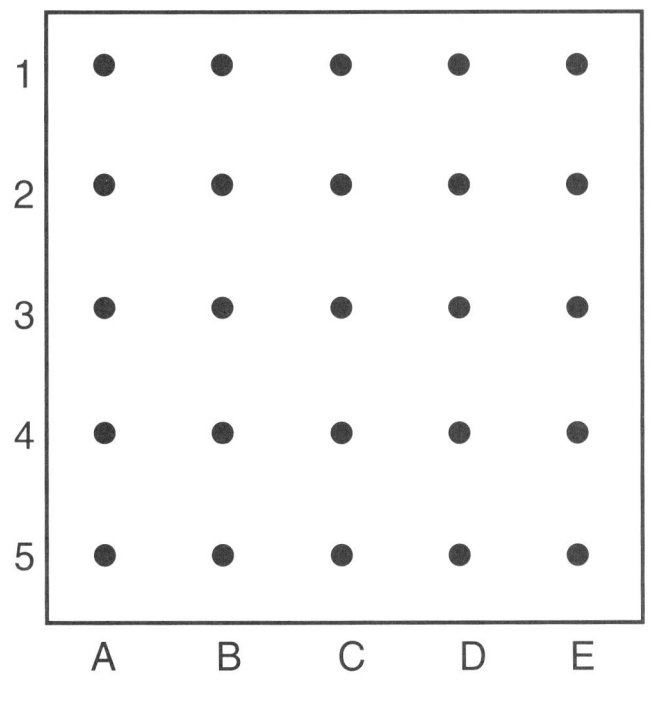
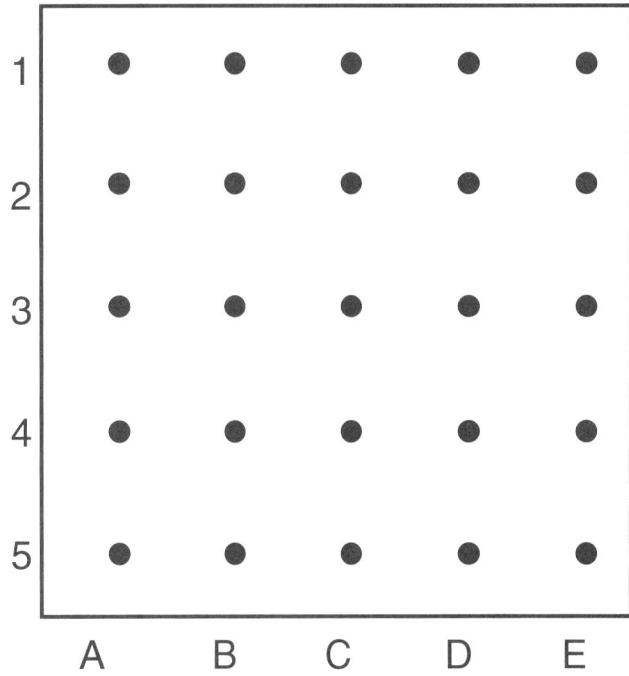

Name _____

Graphing

Graphing

Ask 12 friends which of these four fruits do they like most? Fill in the graph to find out. Color one box on the graph for each vote.

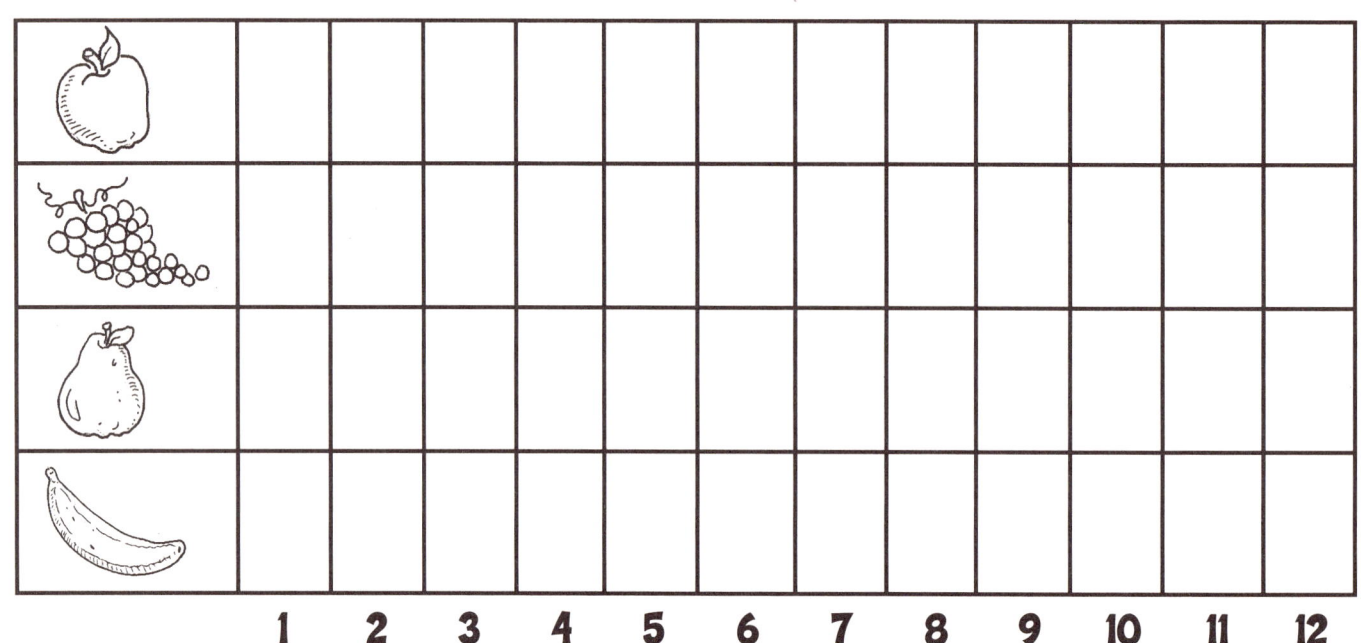

Which fruit was the most popular? _____

How many votes did it get? _____

Which fruit was the least popular? _____

How many votes did it get? _____

If two fruits got the same amount of votes, they "tied." Write any ties below.

_____ and _____

_____ and _____

Name _____

Measuring Length

Measuring Length

Follow these instructions and use a ruler to finish drawing a house.

1. On the right side of the floor, draw a wall 4 inches tall.

2. Draw on a roof. Choose your own style.

3. On the left side of the house, draw the door.
   Make it 2 inches tall and 2 inches wide.

4. On the right side of the house, draw a window.
   Make it 1 inch tall and 3 inches wide.

5. Add a window to the door. Make it 1 inch long and 1 inch wide.

6. Decorate the house any way you choose.

Name _____

Measuring Volume, Fractions

Measuring Volume

Look at each large measuring container. Color in the number of smaller measurements that will equal the larger one.

1 cup = _____ 1/8 cups

 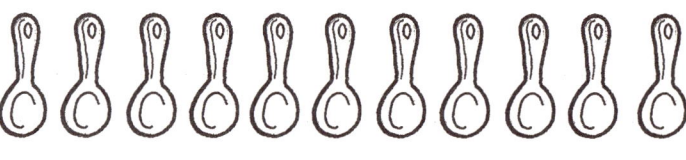

1 teaspoon = _____ 1/8 teaspoons

Which liquid measurement is larger? Circle the larger one.

1 cup or 1 teaspoon   1/2 cup or 1/4 cup   1/2 teaspoon or 1/8 teaspoon

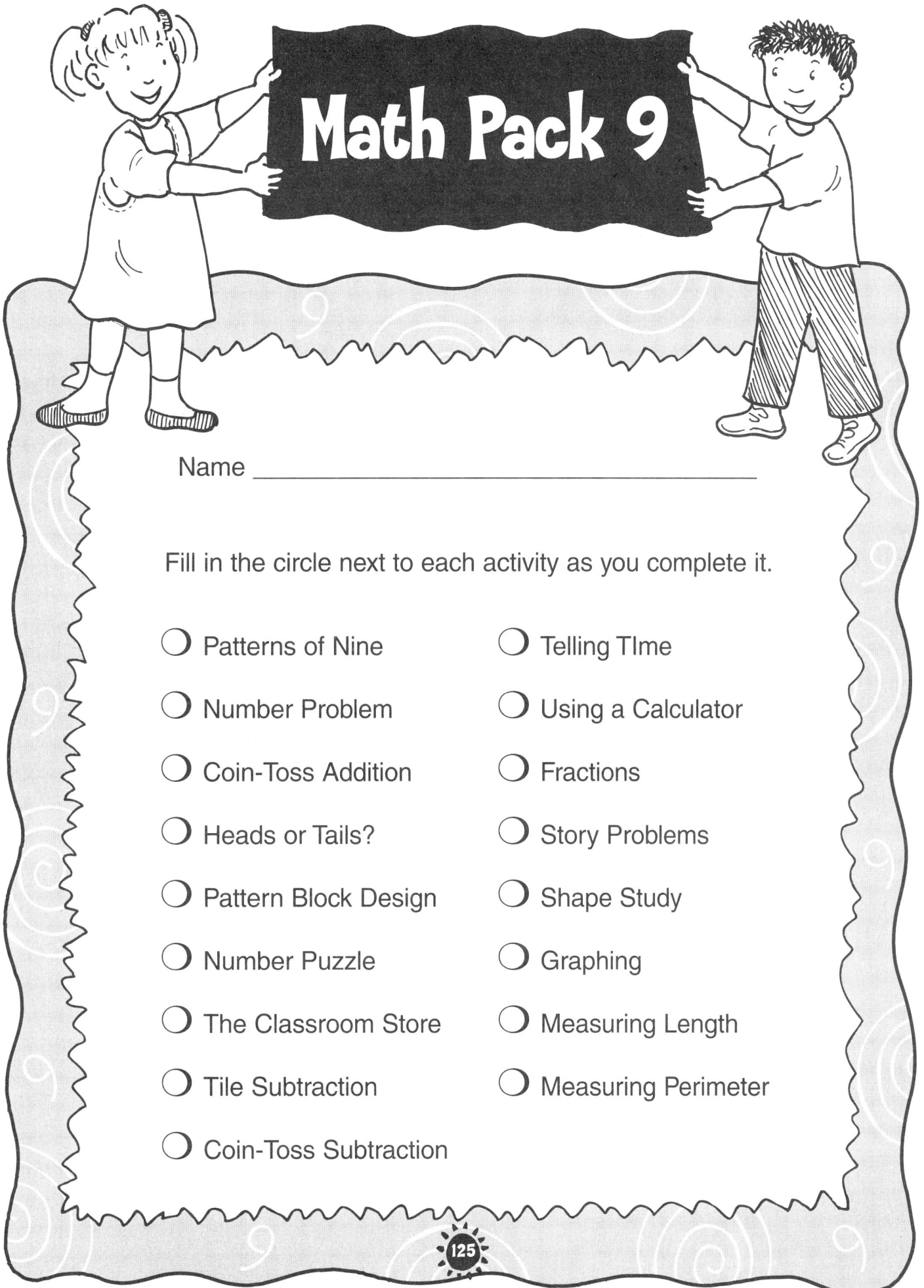

Math Pack 9

Name _____

Fill in the circle next to each activity as you complete it.

- ○ Patterns of Nine
- ○ Number Problem
- ○ Coin-Toss Addition
- ○ Heads or Tails?
- ○ Pattern Block Design
- ○ Number Puzzle
- ○ The Classroom Store
- ○ Tile Subtraction
- ○ Coin-Toss Subtraction

- ○ Telling TIme
- ○ Using a Calculator
- ○ Fractions
- ○ Story Problems
- ○ Shape Study
- ○ Graphing
- ○ Measuring Length
- ○ Measuring Perimeter

Name _____

Recognizing Patterns

Patterns of Nine

1. Look at the number chart.
   Start at 1 and count up to 9.
   Color the number 9. Count 9 more
   squares. Color the 9th number again.
   Keep going. What pattern do you
   see? Talk about it with a classmate.

Hundred's Chart

1	2	3	4	5	6	7	8	9	10
11	12	13	14	15	16	17	18	19	20
21	22	23	24	25	26	27	28	29	30
31	32	33	34	35	36	37	38	39	40
41	42	43	44	45	46	47	48	49	50
51	52	53	54	55	56	57	58	59	60
61	62	63	64	65	66	67	68	69	70
71	72	73	74	75	76	77	78	79	80
81	82	83	84	85	86	87	88	89	90
91	92	93	94	95	96	97	98	99	100

2. Look at the hands below. Each pair of hands is holding up 9 fingers. Imagine that the lowered finger is a space separating the tens and ones. Count the fingers to the left of the lowered finger and to the right of the lowered finger and write the number. The first two have been done for you.

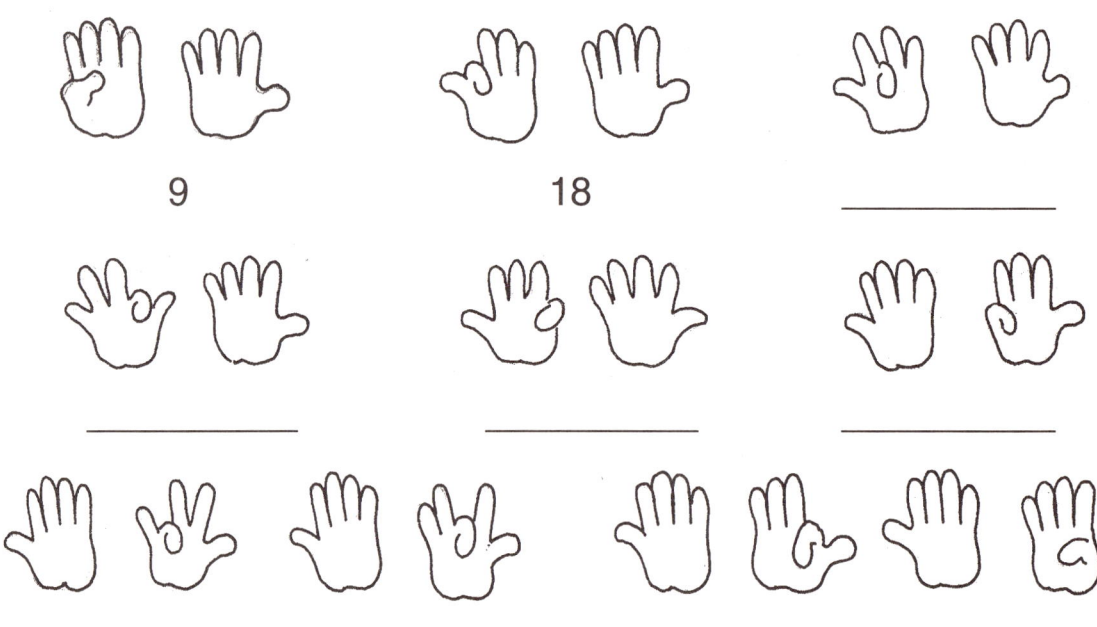

Look at the numbers you wrote. Compare these with the numbers you colored in the chart. What do you notice? Write your ideas on the back.

Name _____   **Addition**

Number Problem

Look at the equation below.

    $5 + 4 = 9$

Make up a story to go with the equation.

Draw a picture in the box to go with your story.

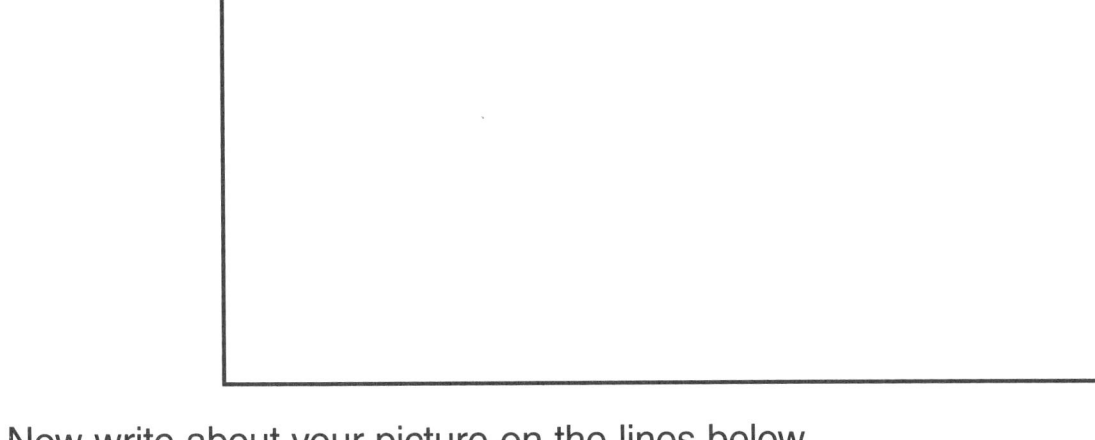

Now write about your picture on the lines below.

_____

_____

_____

_____

Name _____

Adding 9

Coin-Toss Addition

Toss 9 coins. Write "H" for heads or "T" for tails in the circles below to show your toss. Then write the addition equation. Write the number of "heads" first. We did the first one for you. Try it three times.

Equation: _____ 5 + 4 = 9 _____

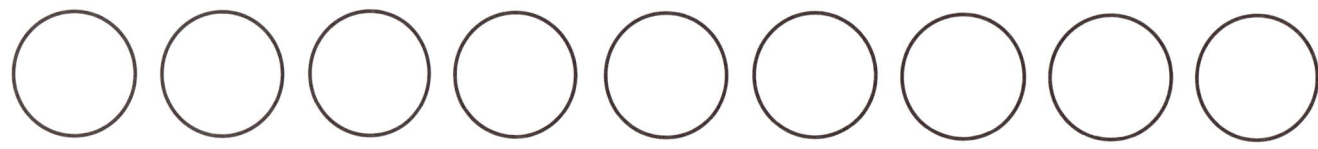

Equation: _____

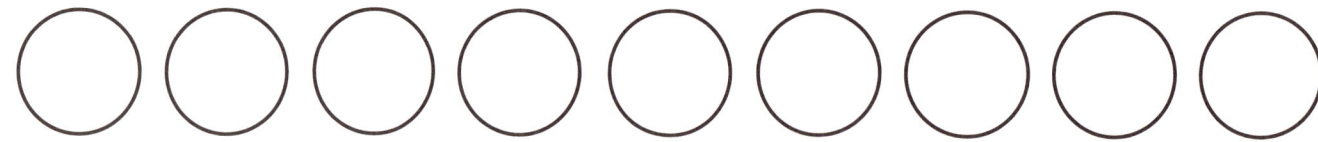

Equation: _____

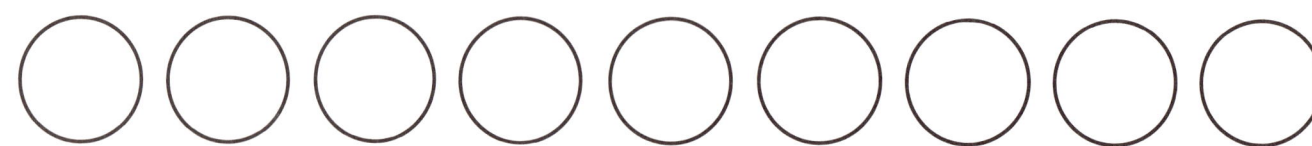

Equation: _____

Name _____

Heads or Tails?

Toss 9 pennies. Look at how the coins landed. Which equation below does it match? Color in the lowest box on the chart in the column for that equation. Toss 9 pennies again and again until one whole column has been colored. This is the combination of coins you tossed the most.

0¢ + 9¢	1¢ + 8¢	2¢ + 7¢	3¢ + 6¢	4¢ + 5¢	5¢ + 4¢	6¢ + 3¢	7¢ + 2¢	8¢ + 1¢	9¢ + 0¢
heads tails	heads tails	heads tails	heads tails	heads tails	heads tails	heads tails	heads tails	heads tails	heads tails

Probability, Adding

Name _____

Creative Thinking

Pattern Block Design

How many total pieces are in this pattern block design? 2 + 2 + 5 = _____

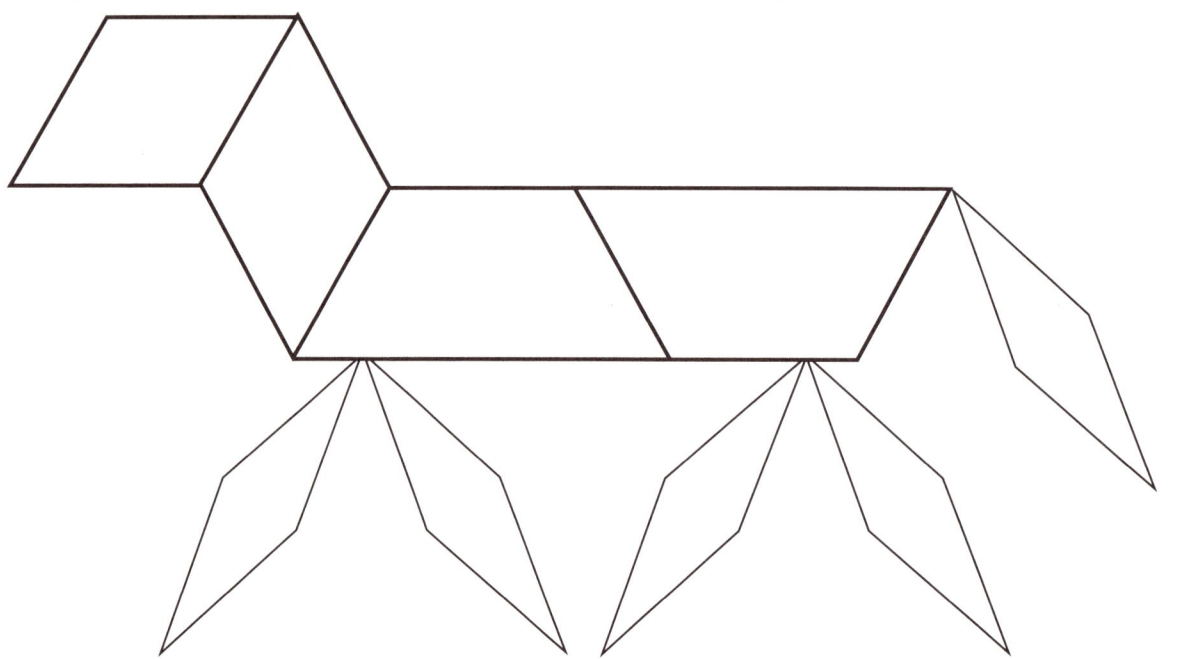

Now make your own design. Use 9 pattern blocks from the pattern block page. Cut out the shapes and trace or glue them in the space below. You may need to use a shape more than once.

Write an equation to show how many of each shape you used.

Equation: _____

Name _____

Adding, Money

Number Puzzle

These boxes form the number 9.
Write a number in each box.
You can use 0, 1, 2, 3, 4, 5, 6, 7, 8, or 9
The sum of each row should equal 9.
The sum of each column should equal 9.

The Classroom Store

Look at what is for sale in the class store. You have to spend 9¢. You should only buy 1 thing, 2 things, or 3 things. Color what you will buy.

Write an equation to show what you bought.

_____

Which coins will you give the store clerk? Color them in.

Name _____

Subtracting 9

Tile Subtraction

Take 9 tiles. Ask a classmate to hide some in his or her hand. Color the squares below to show how many are left. Write a subtraction equation to find out how many tiles your classmate is hiding. We did the first one for you. Try it four times.

Equation: _____9 - 3 = 6_____

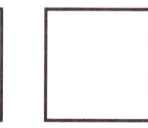

Equation: _____

Equation: _____

Equation: _____

Equation: _____

Name _____   **Subtracting 9**

Coin-Toss Subtraction

Toss 9 coins. Write "H" for heads or "T" for tails in the circles below to show how the coins landed. Then finish each sentence to tell about your toss. Write a subtraction equation to show your toss, too. Write the number of "heads" first. We did the first one for you. Try it two times.

"H"=Heads   "T"=Tails

There are ____fewer____ heads than tails.
        (more/fewer)

Subtraction equation: __9 coins__ - __4 heads__ = __5 tails__

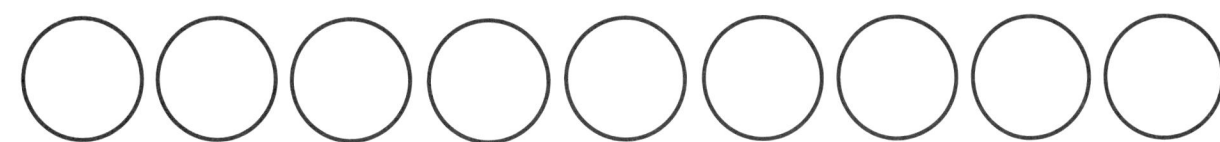

There are _____ heads than tails.
        (more/fewer)

Subtraction equation: _____ - _____ = _____

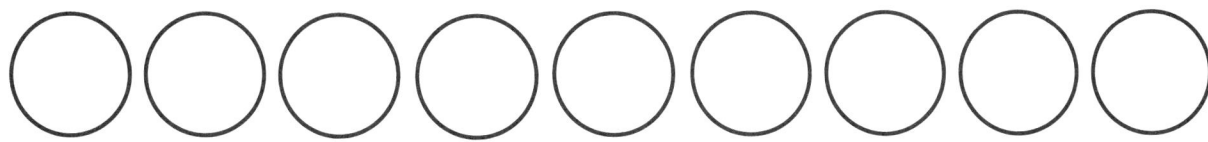

There are _____ heads than tails.
        (more/fewer)

Subtraction equation: _____ - _____ = _____

Name _____

Time, Calculator

Telling Time

Draw the hands on the clock so it shows 9:00.

Draw the hands on the clock so it shows 9:30.

What time was it 1/2 hour before 9:00?

_____

What time was it 1/2 hour after 9:30?

_____

Using a Calculator

Solve the equations below. Check your answers with a calculator.

Add:

7 + 2 = _____   1 + 8 = _____

5 + 3 = _____   2 + 6 = _____

4 + 5 = _____   0 + 9 = _____

6 + 3 = _____   1 + 6 = _____

5 + 4 = _____   2 + 7 = _____

Subtract:

8 - 6 = _____   9 - 2 = _____

7 - 4 = _____   8 - 6 = _____

9 - 1 = _____   9 - 5 = _____

9 - 4 = _____   9 - 8 = _____

9 - 3 = _____   4 - 2 = _____

Name _____

Fractions, Critical Thinking

Fractions

A fraction has two numbers. The top number tells you how many parts to color. The bottom number tells you how many total parts there are.

Color 1/9 of the circle red.
Color 8/9 of the circle blue.

Color 5/9 of the rectangle red.
Color 3/9 of the rectangle green.
Color 1/9 of the rectangle blue.

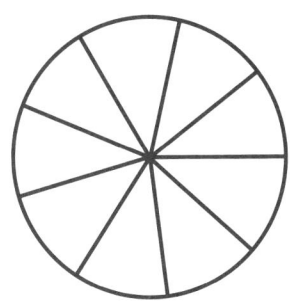

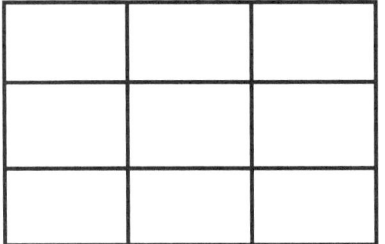

1/9 + 8/9 = 9/9

5/9 + 3/9 + 1/9 = 9/9

Look at the 2 sets of dogs. Solve the fraction equation.

$$\frac{5}{9} + \frac{4}{9} = \frac{}{}$$

Look at the 3 sets of cats. Complete the fraction equation.

_____ + _____ + _____ = ——

Name _____

Problem Solving

Story Problems

Solve these story problems.
Cut out the butterflies at the bottom of the page to help you.

1. A.J. saw 9 butterflies sitting on a log.
   He ran up to them and 7 flew away.
   How many butterflies were left? _____

2. Austin saw 5 butterflies flying.
   He saw 4 butterflies sitting on a log.
   How many butterflies did he see in all? _____

3. Frankie watched 9 butterflies on a log.
   3 butterflies were monarchs. The rest were swallowtails.
   How many swallowtails did Frankie see? _____

Name _____

Identifying Shapes

Shape Study

A nonagon has 9 sides. On a nonagon, all the sides are the same length.

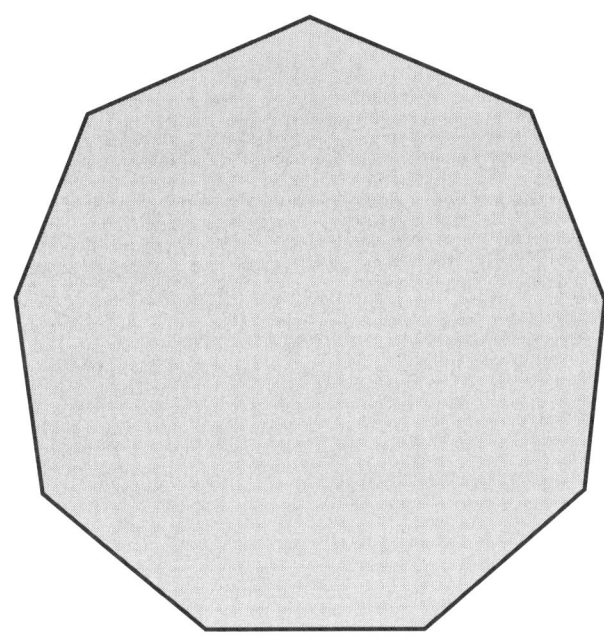

Connect the dots in the geoboards below to make other shapes with 9 sides.

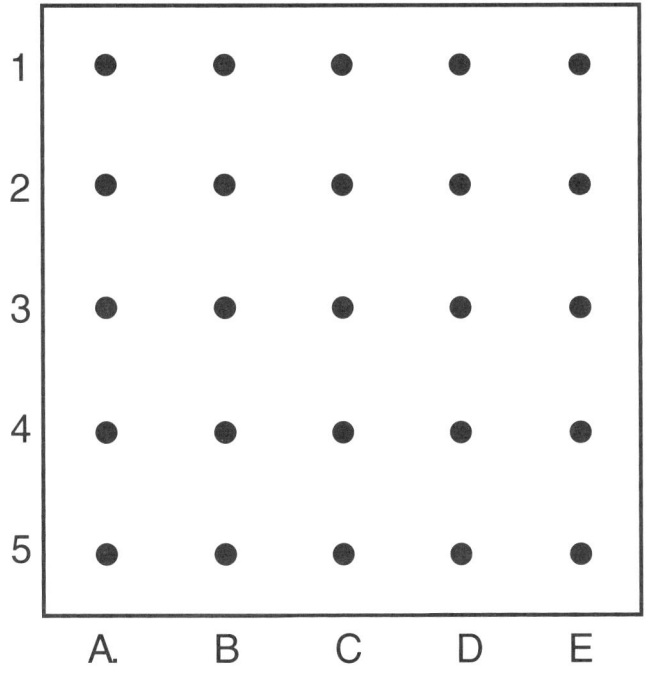
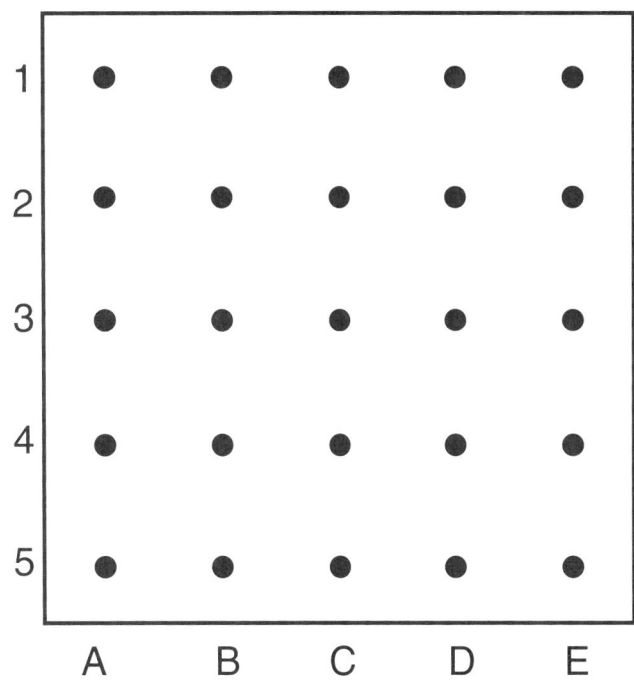

Name _____

Graphing

Graphing

Read the words at the bottom of the graph. Count how many of each is in your classroom. Color in the correct number of boxes on the chart.

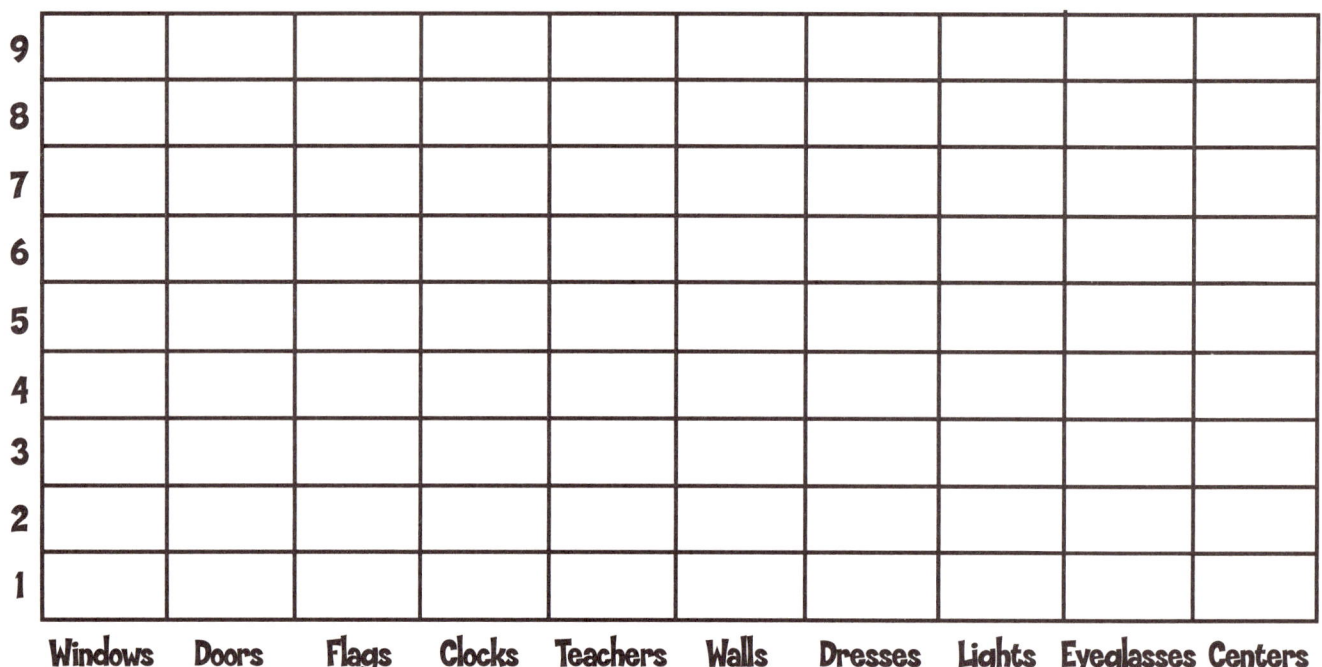

Are there more teachers or centers? _____

Are there more windows or lights? _____

Are there fewer doors or flags? _____

Are there fewer clocks or walls? _____

Are there more eyeglasses or bookshelves or flags? _____

Are there fewer windows or doors or clocks? _____

Which object is there most of? _____

Which object is there least of? _____

Name _____

Measuring Length

Measuring Length

People didn't always measure with rulers. Long ago, Egyptians and other peoples measured objects with body parts. Try it!

A "digit" is the width of your middle finger at the top joint where it bends. How many digits long is:

a pair of scissors? _____

a math book? _____

a crayon? _____

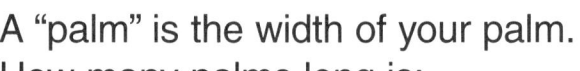

A "palm" is the width of your palm. How many palms long is:

a math book? _____

your desk? _____

a ruler? _____

A "span" is the length from the tip of your pinkie to the tip of your thumb when your hand is wide open. How many spans long is:

your desk? _____

the teacher's desk? _____

a door? _____

Name _____

Measuring Perimeter

Measuring Perimeter

Use the inch side of a ruler and measure each side of each shape. Write the inches in the spaces below. Then add up all the sides to find the perimeter, or distance, around each shape.

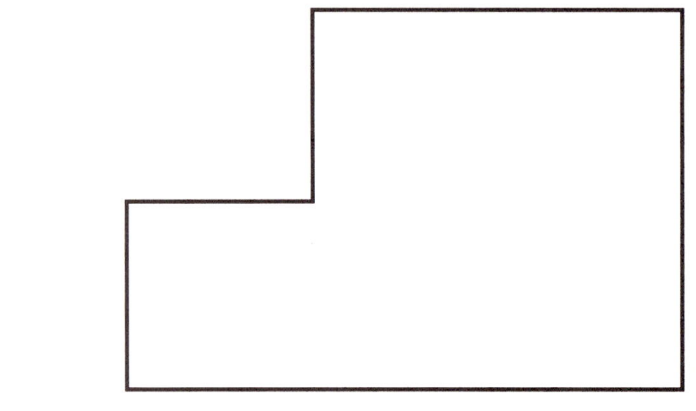

____ + ____ + ____ + ____ + ____ + ____ = ____ inches

____ + ____ + ____ + ____ + ____ + ____ + ____ + ____ = ____ inches

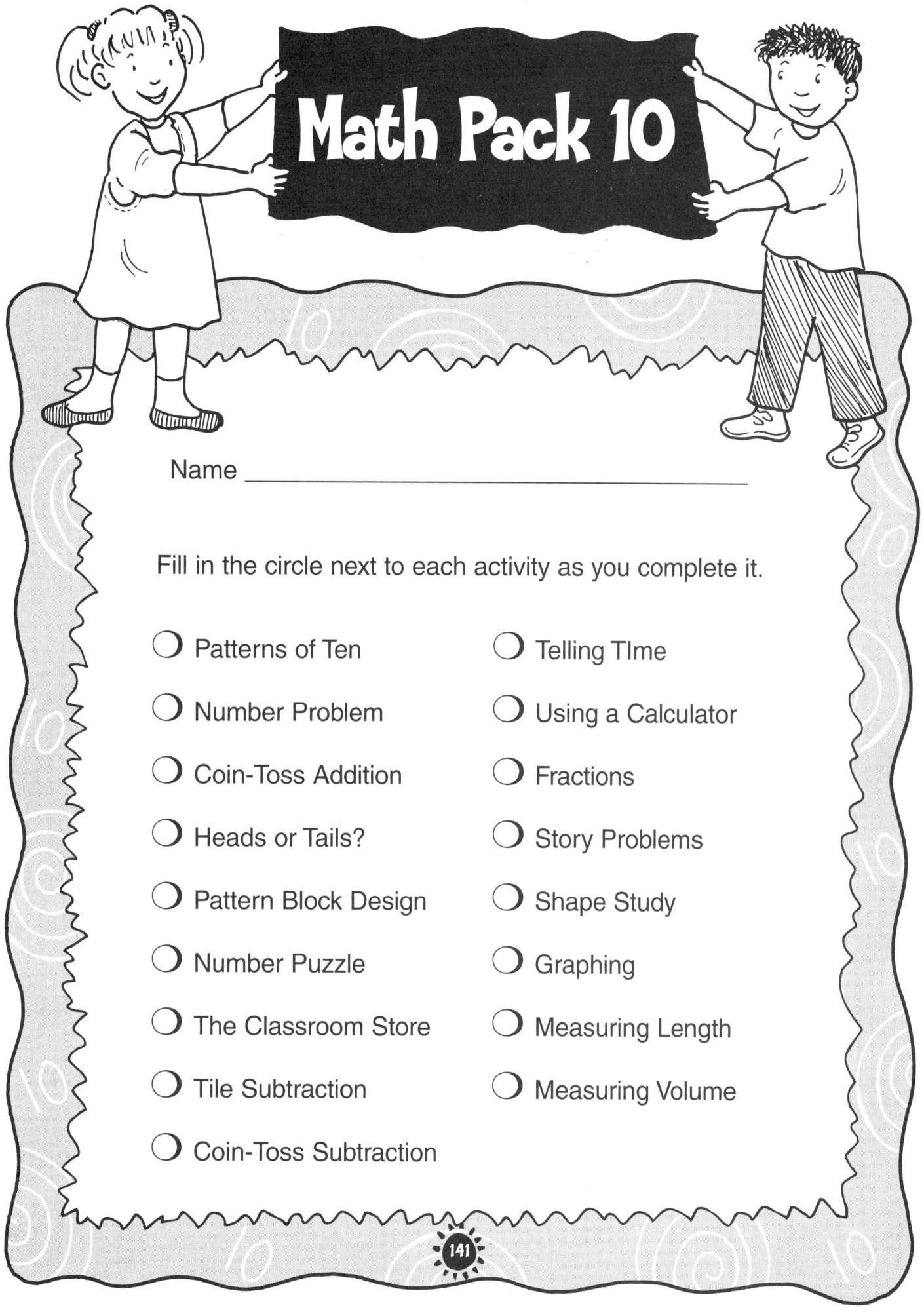

Name _____

Recognizing Patterns

Patterns of Ten

1. Look at the number chart below. Start at 1 and count up to 10. Color the number 10. Count 10 more squares. Color the 10th number again. Keep going!

Hundred's Chart

1	2	3	4	5	6	7	8	9	10
11	12	13	14	15	16	17	18	19	20
21	22	23	24	25	26	27	28	29	30
31	32	33	34	35	36	37	38	39	40
41	42	43	44	45	46	47	48	49	50
51	52	53	54	55	56	57	58	59	60
61	62	63	64	65	66	67	68	69	70
71	72	73	74	75	76	77	78	79	80
81	82	83	84	85	86	87	88	89	90
91	92	93	94	95	96	97	98	99	100

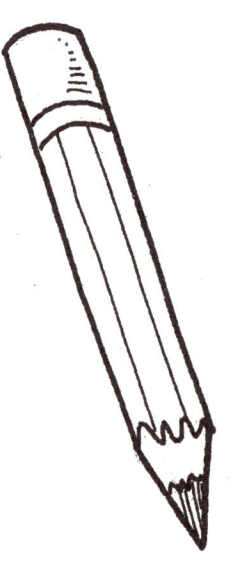

What pattern do you see? Talk about it with a classmate.

2. Think about things that come in 10's. List or draw them below. (Hint: Your hands will give you a clue!)

Name _____

Addition

Number Problem

Look at the equation below.

7 + 3 = 10

Make up a story to go with the equation.

Draw a picture in the box to go with your story.

Now write about your picture on the lines below.

_____

_____

_____

_____

Name _____

Adding 10

Coin-Toss Addition

Toss 10 coins. Write "H" for heads or "T" for tails in the circles below to show your toss. Then write the addition equation. Write the number of "heads" first. We did the first one for you. Try it three times.

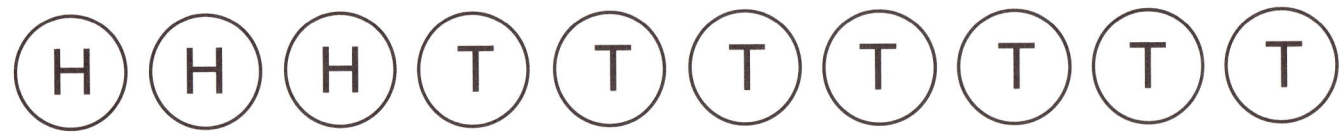

Equation: _____ 3 + 7 = 10 _____

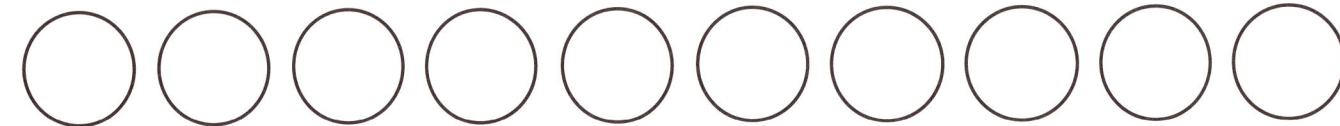

Equation: _____

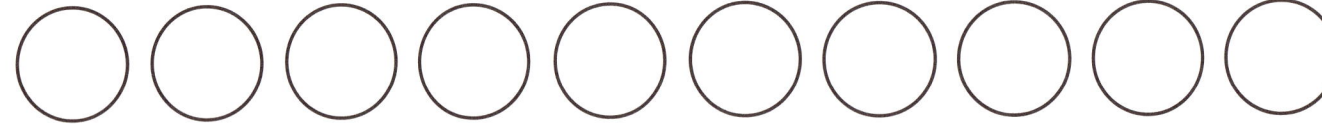

Equation: _____

Equation: _____

144

Name _____

Heads or Tails?

Toss 10 pennies. Look at how the coins landed. Which equation below does it match? Color in the lowest box on the chart in the column for that equation. Toss 10 pennies again and again until one whole column has been colored. This is the combination of coins you tossed the most.

Probability. Adding

| 0¢ + 10¢ | 1¢ + 9¢ | 2¢ + 8¢ | 3¢ + 7¢ | 4¢ + 6¢ | 5¢ + 5¢ | 6¢ + 4¢ | 7¢ + 3¢ | 8¢ + 2¢ | 9¢ + 1¢ | 10¢ + 0¢ |
| heads tails | heads tails | heads tails | heads tails | heads tails | heads tails | heads tails | heads tails | heads tails | heads tails | heads tails |

Name _____

Creative Thinking

Pattern Block Design

How many total pieces are in this pattern block design? 2 + 2 + 2 + 4 = _____

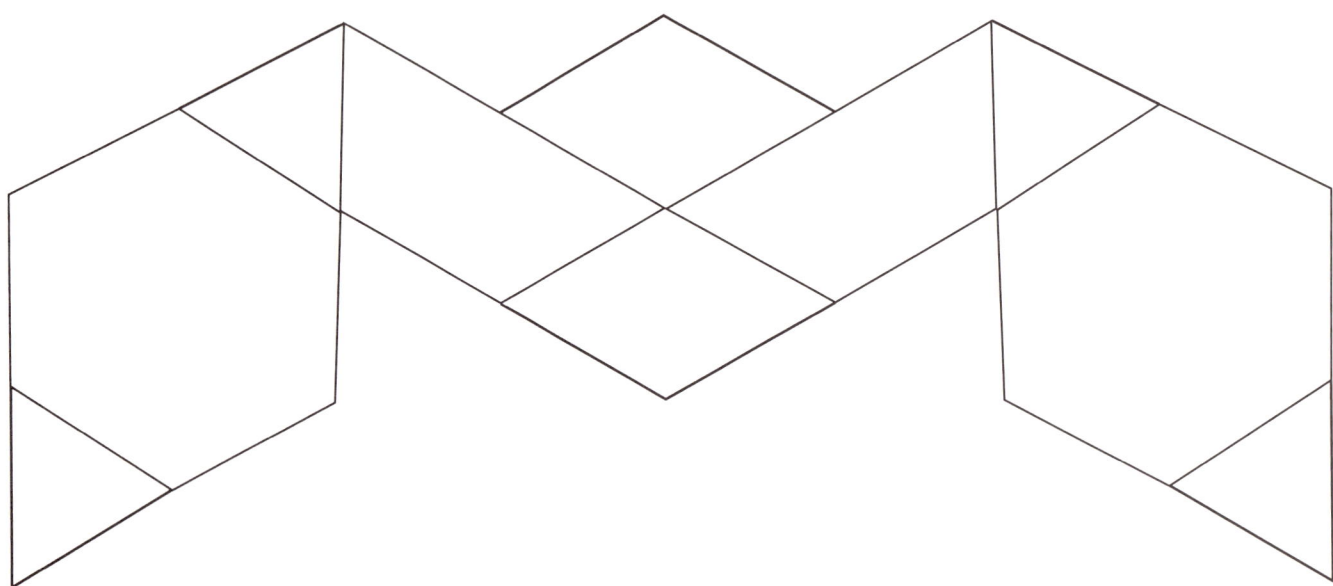

Now make your own design. Use 10 pattern blocks from the pattern block page. Cut out the shapes and trace or glue them in the space below. You may need to use a shape more than once.

Write an equation to show how many of each shape you used.

Equation: _____

Name _____

Adding, Money

Number Puzzle

These boxes form the number 10.
Write a number in each box.
You can use 0, 1, 2, 3, 4, 5, 6, 7, 8, 9, or 10.
The sum of each row should equal 10.
The sum of each column should equal 10.

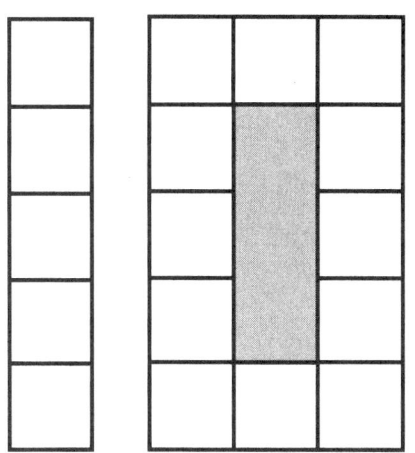

The Classroom Store

Look at what is for sale in the classroom store. You have to spend 10¢.
You should only buy 1 thing, 2 things, 3 things or 4 things. Color what you will buy.

1¢    2¢ 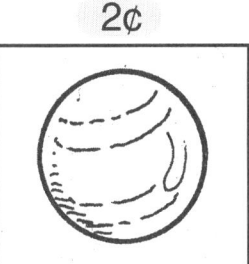   3¢    4¢    5¢

6¢    7¢    8¢    9¢ 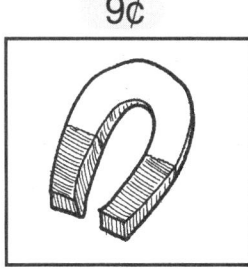   10¢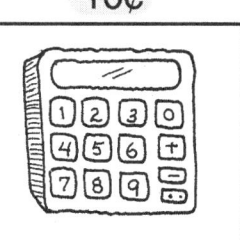

Write an equation to show what you bought.

_____

Which coins will you give the store clerk? _____

Subtracting 10

Name _____

Tile Subtraction

Take 10 tiles. Ask a classmate to hide some in his or her hand. Color the squares below to show how many tiles are left. Write the subtraction equation to find out how many tiles your classmate is hiding. We did the first one for you. Try it five times.

Equation: __10 - 2 = 8__   Equation: _____

Equation: _____   Equation: _____

Equation: _____   Equation: _____

Name _____

Subtracting 10

Coin-Toss Subtraction

Toss 10 coins. Write "H" for heads or "T" for tails in the circles below to show how the coins landed. Then finish each sentence to tell about your toss. Write a subtraction equation to show your toss, too. Write the number of "heads first." We did the first one for you. Try it two times.

"H"=Heads   "T"=Tails

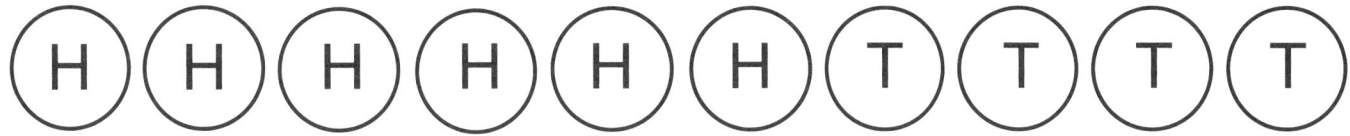

There are ____more____ heads than tails.
(more/fewer)

Subtraction equation: __10 coins__ - __6 heads__ = __4 tails__

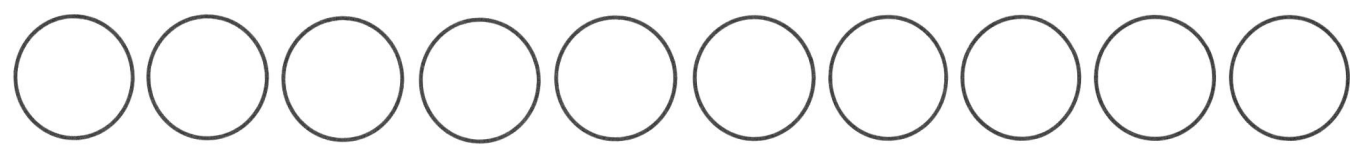

There are _____ heads than tails.
(more/fewer)

Subtraction equation: _____ - _____ = _____

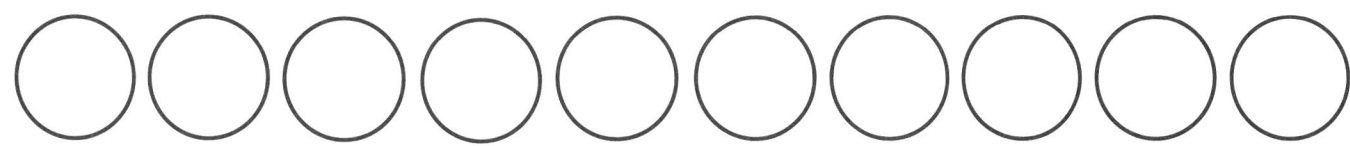

There are _____ heads than tails.
(more/fewer)

Subtraction equation: _____ - _____ = _____

Name _____

Time, Calculator

Telling Time

Draw the hands on the clock so it shows 10:00.

Draw the hands on the clock so it shows 10:30.

What do you do at 10:00 in the morning?

_____

Using a Calculator

Solve the equations below. Check your answers with a calculator.

Add:

5 + 5 = _____   2 + 7 = _____
4 + 5 = _____   2 + 8 = _____
6 + 4 = _____   9 + 1 = _____
3 + 5 = _____   7 + 1 = _____
7 + 3 = _____   10 + 0 = _____

Subtract:

10 - 7 = _____   10 - 1 = _____
10 - 9 = _____   10 - 3 = _____
10 - 5 = _____   10 - 6 = _____
9 - 6 = _____   8 - 5 = _____
7 - 6 = _____   10 - 10 = _____

Name _____

Fractions, Critical Thinking

Fractions

A fraction has two numbers. The top number will tell you how many parts to color. The bottom number tells you how many total parts there are.

$\frac{10}{10}$ is the whole circle.

Color $\frac{8}{10}$ of the circle.

How much is not colored? _____

$\frac{10}{10}$ is the whole rectangle.

Color $\frac{4}{10}$ of the rectangle.

How much is not colored? _____

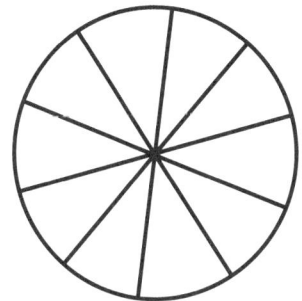

$\frac{10}{10} - \frac{8}{10} = \frac{}{}$

$\frac{10}{10} - \frac{4}{10} = \frac{}{}$

Solve this fraction equation. Cross out the dogs to help you.

$\frac{10}{10} - \frac{3}{10} = \frac{}{}$

Name _____

Problem Solving

Story Problems

Solve these story problems. Cut out the gumballs at the bottom of the page to help you.

1. Shauna likes green gumballs. She bought 10 gumballs. Only 2 were green. How many gumballs were not green? _____

2. Leon had 3 yellow gumballs. He also had 2 white gumballs and 1 green one. He had 4 pink gumballs, too. How many gumballs did he have in all? _____

3. Davis brought 10 gumballs to school. He gave 2 to Tracy. He gave 3 to Maya. How many gumballs did Davis still have? _____

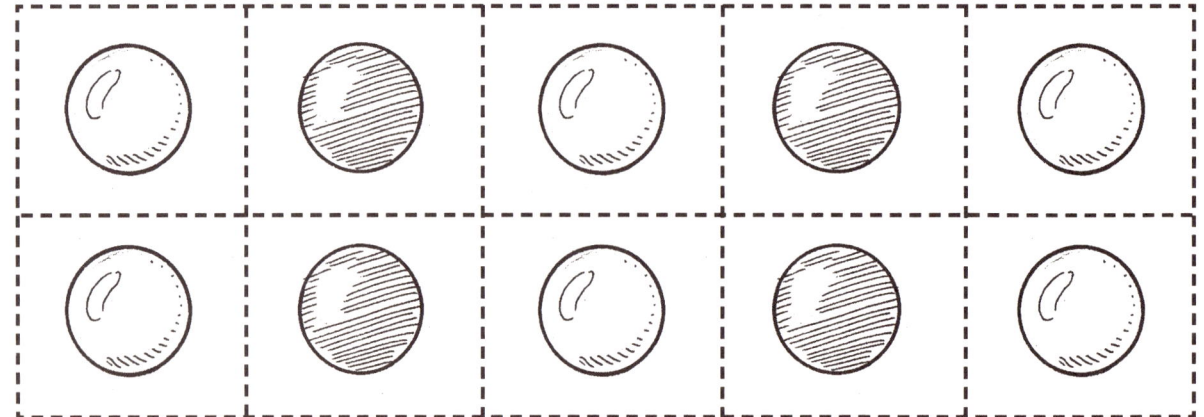

Name _____

Identifying Shapes

Shape Study

A decagon has 10 sides. On a decagon, all the sides are the same length.

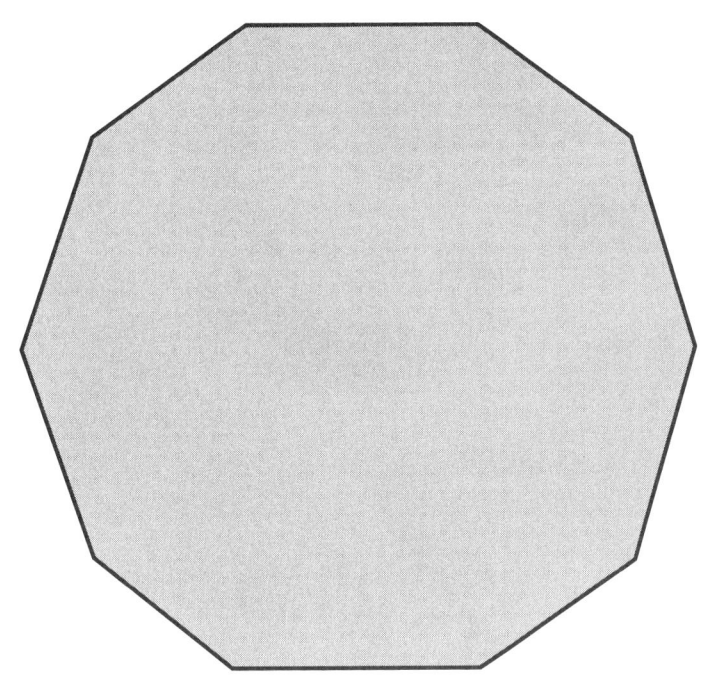

Connect the dots in the geoboards below to make other shapes with 10 sides.

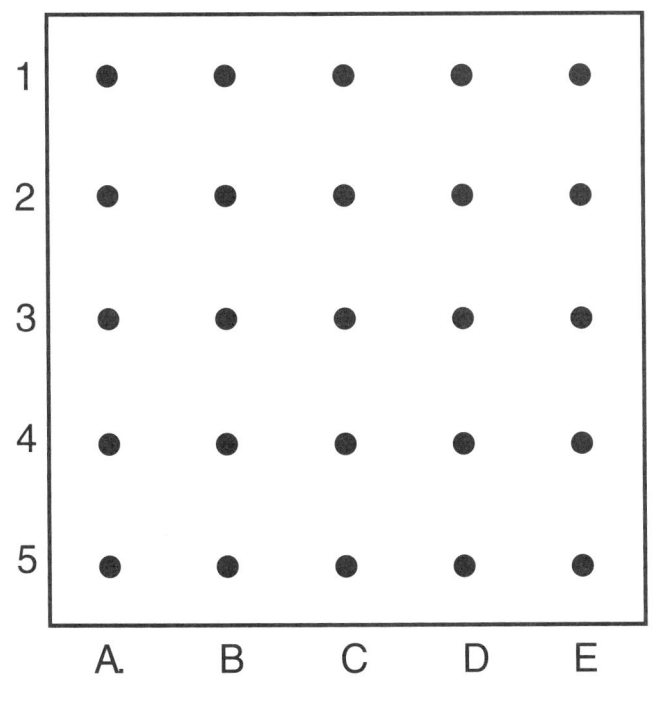
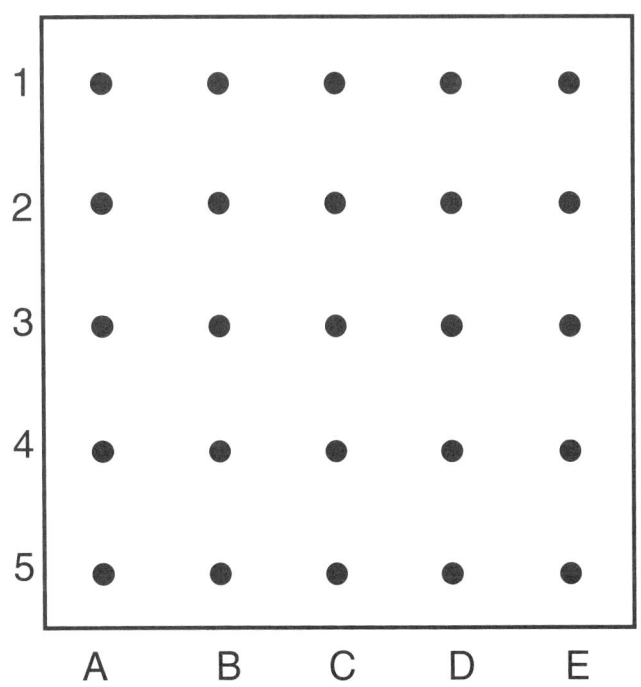

Name _____

Graphing, Money

Graphing

How many pennies equal 5¢? Color in the boxes on the graph to show your answer. How many nickels equal 5¢? Color in the boxes on the graph to show your answer.

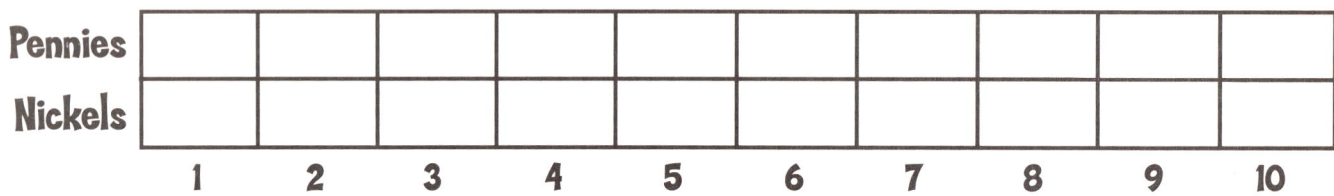

How many pennies equal 10¢? Color in the boxes on the graph to show your answer. How many nickels equal 10¢? Color in the boxes on the graph to show your answer. How many dimes equal 10¢? Color in the boxes on the graph to show your answer.

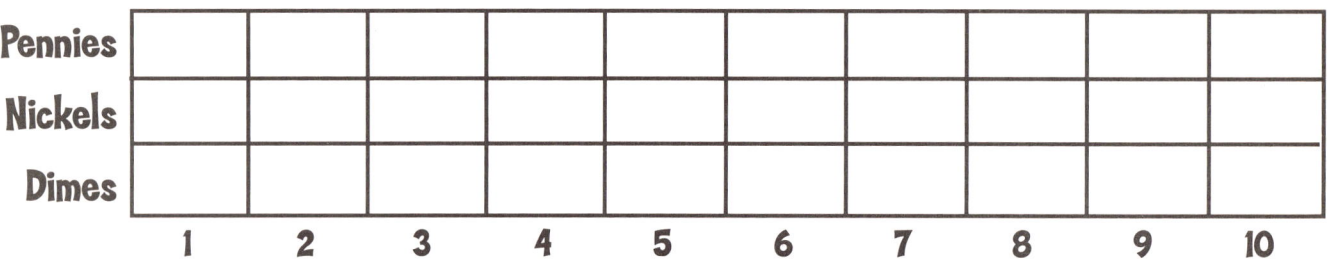

How many pennies equal 25¢? Color in the boxes on the graph to show your answer. How many nickels equal 25¢? Color in the boxes on the graph to show your answer. How many quarters equal 25¢? Color in the boxes on the graph to show your answer.

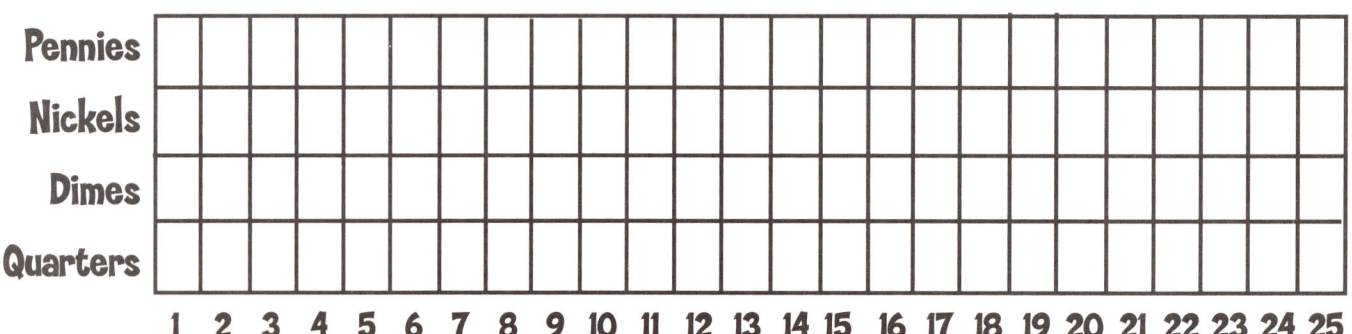

Name _____

Measuring Length

Measuring Length

People didn't always measure with rulers. Long ago, Egyptians and other peoples measured objects with body parts. Try it!

A "cubit" is the length from the elbow to the top of the middle finger. How many cubits long is:

a table? _____

a chalkboard? _____

a coat rack? _____

A "stature" is your height, or the length of your arms open wide. How many statures long is:

a chalkboard? _____

a coat rack? _____

a wall? _____

When could using Egyptian measurements be helpful?

_____

_____

Why isn't this usually the best way to measure things?

_____

Talk about your answers with a classmate.

Name _____

Measuring Volume, Fractions

Measuring Volume

The recipe below explains how to make peanut-butter balls. Read the recipe. Then answer the questions.

Peanut-Butter Balls

Ingredients:

2 cups peanut butter
2 cups graham cracker crumbs
2 cups powdered sugar
1/4 cup warm butter
*Optional: additional 1/8 cup of powered sugar (separate)

Directions:

1. Mix all the ingredients together (except the optional powdered sugar).
2. Roll into balls, about the size of a quarter.
3. Optional: Roll the balls in the 1/8 cup of powdered sugar.
4. Chill for 2 hours.

Several classmates want to help make the peanut-butter balls.

1. How many students would be needed if each measured 1/2 cup of the peanut butter?

   _____

2. How many students would be needed if each measured 1/4 cup of the graham cracker crumbs?

   _____

3. How many students would be needed if each measured 1/3 cup of the powdered sugar?

   _____

Math Packs Appendix

Pattern Block Shapes

Student Survey

Student Self-Evaluation

Assessment

End-of-Year Test

End-of-Year Test Answer Key

Square Flashcards

Math Packs Answer Key

Name _____

Pattern Block Shapes

Use the pattern block shapes on this page for the pattern-block activities.

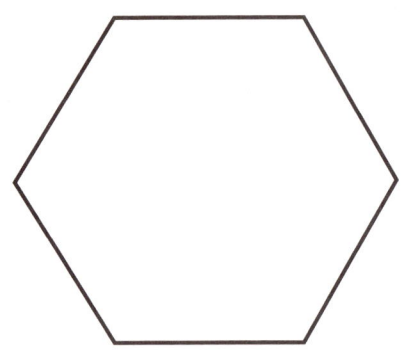 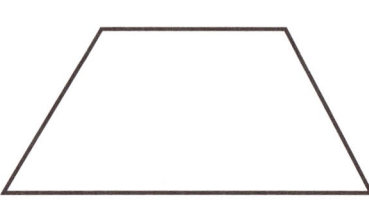 

 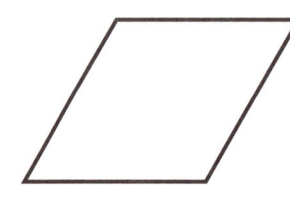 

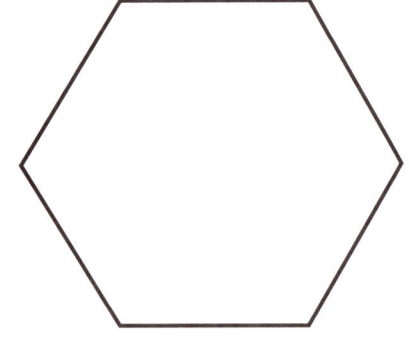 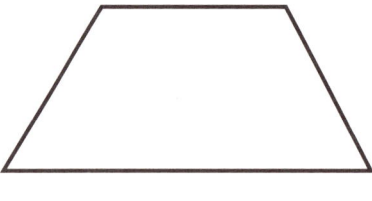 

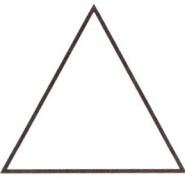  

Name _____

Student Survey

Color in a circle to show how you feel.

This is how I feel about:

	great	okay	sad
Math Pack activities	☺	😐	☹
how good I am at math	☺	😐	☹
using "things" to help me learn	☺	😐	☹
story problems	☺	😐	☹
counting by 1s, 2s, 5s, 10s	☺	😐	☹
adding and subtracting	☺	😐	☹
measuring things	☺	😐	☹
working with shapes	☺	😐	☹
reading a graph	☺	😐	☹
making predictions	☺	😐	☹
figuring out number patterns	☺	😐	☹

appendix

Name _____

Student Self-Evaluation

Fill in the blank below. Then color in some stars at the bottom to show how much you've learned!

I have completed Math Pack _____ on _____

I learned _____
_____
_____

I did well at _____
_____
_____

I need to practice _____
_____
_____

I give myself

Name _____

Assessment

Give each student a checkmark after each Math Pack activity has been completed. In the last column, indicate if the activity was completed individually (I), with a partner (P), in a small group (G), or as a whole class activity (W).

Child's Name: _____   Date: _____

Math Pack: _____

Addition

	✓–	✓	✓+	
Number Problems				
Coin-Toss Addition				
Heads or Tails?				
Pattern Block Design				
Number Puzzle				
The Classroom Store				
Using a Calculator				

Subtraction

	✓–	✓	✓+	
Tile Subtraction				
Coin-Toss Subtraction				
Using a Calculator				

Other Concepts

	✓–	✓	✓+	
Patterns				
Money				
Fractions				
Story Problems				
Time				
Graphing				
Shapes				
Measurement, Length				
Measurement, Volume				
Measurement, Perimeter				

End-of-Year Test

Name _____ Grade _____

Teacher _____ Date _____

School _____ District _____

• •

PROBLEM SOLVING

Use the calendar to answer each question.

April						
Sunday	Monday	Tuesday	Wednesday	Thursday	Friday	Saturday
1	2	3	4	5	6	7
8	9	10	11	12	13	14

1. Rosa's birthday is the second Monday in April. The date is April _____

2. Today is Friday, April 6th. What will the date be in one week? April _____

3. Here are the months all mixed up:

   March   May   June   July   December   September   August
   January   October   November   February   April

   Which is the 12th month of the year? _____

4. There are 18 kites flying above the beach.
   7 blue kites land on the beach.
   Then 1 more lands on the beach.
   How many kites stayed up in the air?
   Draw the kites in the box.
   Then write the equation on the line below the box.

Equation: _____

5. There are 7 blue kites, 5 red kites, and 6 yellow kites. Graph them below.

Blue

Red

Yellow

6. Which color kites are there the least of? _____

CONCEPT OF NUMBERS

7. How many fish? _____.

8. Write the number five hundred twenty six: _____.

9. Finish counting: 87, 88, _____, _____, _____, _____,

10. Write these numbers below from smallest to largest: 68   149   82

   _____   _____   _____

11. The number 10 is between _____ and _____ on the number line.

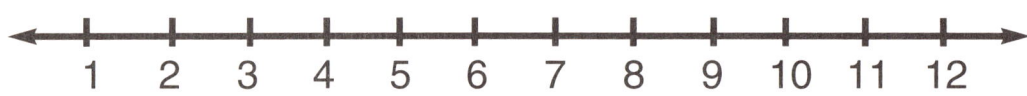

Look at these numbers: 89   570   68   570   139

12. Cross out the numbers that are equal.

13. Now circle the largest number that is left.

14. Put a square around the number that is less than the other numbers.

15. 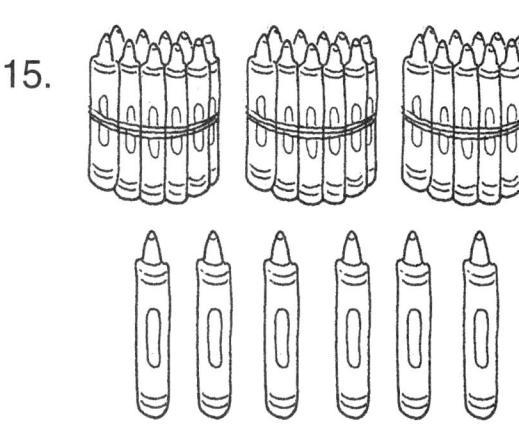 Count the crayons.

How many tens? _____

How many ones? _____

How many crayons all together? _____

16. Count by 2s: _10_ , _12_ , _14_ , ____, ____, ____, ____, ____.

17. Count by 5s: _45_ , _50_ , _55_ , _60_ , ____, ____, ____, ____, ____.

18. Count by 10s: _30_ , _40_ , _50_ , ____, ____, ____, ____, ____.

19. A piece of melon is cut into 6 slices.
    Beth eats 3 slices. Color them red.
    Joe eats 2 slices. Color them blue.

    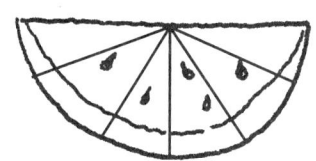

    Who has eaten half? _____.

20. Are there an odd or even number of fish?

    _____.

21. In the number 396, how many groups of 100 are there?

    _____.

COMPUTATION

22. What is the fraction for the part of the flower that has black petals? _____

23. 9 + 1 = _____   24. 5 - 2 = _____   25. 5
                                                  + 3

26. 4   27. 10
    -2   -2

28. There are 60 children in the room and one gumball machine. We need to give everyone one gumball. We begin counting the gumballs. We count 60 and find there are some left. Do we have to count the rest of the gumballs to accomplish our task?

_____

. . . .

MEASUREMENT

29. The first rectangle is _____ inches in length.

30. The first rectangle is _____ inch in width.

31. The second rectangle is _____ centimeters in length.

32. The second rectangle is _____ centimeters in width.

33. The dinosaur is _____ centimeters tall.

34. The bear is about _____ centimeters tall.

35. The _____ is the shortest.

36. The dinosaur is _____ centimeters taller than the bear.

37. Which holds more water?

   _____

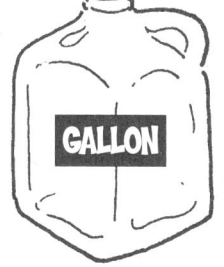

38. What time is it?   39. What time is it?

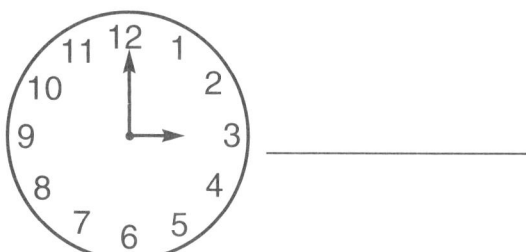 _____   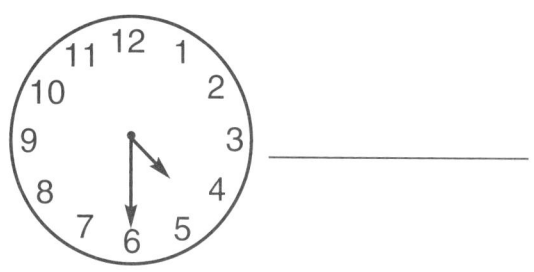 _____

40. The thermometer is marked every 10 degrees.
    Look at the mercury in black.

    The temperature is _____ degrees.

41. To measure around a garbage can,
    would you use a yard stick or a tape measure? _____

42. Count the money.

_____

43. Count the money.

_____

• •

GEOMETRY

44. Draw a line to the sign shaped like a <u>triangle</u>.

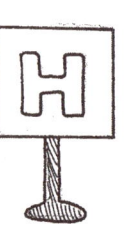

45. Draw a line to the sign shaped like a <u>rectangle</u>.

46. Draw a line to the sign shaped like a <u>circle</u>.

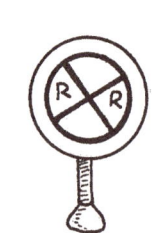

47. Draw a line to the sign shaped like a <u>square</u>.

48. Draw a line to the prism made of <u>rectangles</u>.

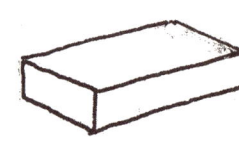

49. Draw a line to the cube made of <u>squares</u>.

50. Draw a line to the cylinder made with a <u>circle</u>.

51. A diamond has _____ sides.

52. An octagon has _____ sides.

53. A trapezoid has _____ sides.

54. A pentagon has _____ sides.

55. Draw the next shape in the pattern.

56. Color blue the line that shows how a piece of yarn would lie on a table.

57. Draw the line of symmetry for this piece of pie.

DATA ANALYSIS

As a morning snack, 9 children ordered milk. Because Sally is allergic to milk, she bought orange juice from the juice machine. 7 other children went to the juice machine and bought cans of apple juice.

58. Graph the data

Favorite Drinks for Snack Time

59. How many fruit juices did they drink altogether?

_____

60. How many more children drank apple juice than orange juice?

_____

61. Which drink was there the least of?

_____

PROBABLILITY

Amy tossed 6 pennies.
All 6 pennies came up tails:

Todd also tossed 6 pennies.
There were 3 heads and 3 tails.

62. Which toss does not happen often:

    a. Amy's   or   b. Todd's

63. If you tossed 100 pennies, which of these would <u>not</u> happen very often?

    a. 98 heads   and   2 tails

    b. 48 heads   and   52 tails

• •

FUNCTIONS AND ALGEBRA

64. Draw the next shape in the pattern.

65. Which is the formula for the pattern in question 65?

    a. AB   b. ABC   c. ABD   d. ABB   e. AAB

66. It rained for 3 days this month and 20 days last month. How many days did it rain in both months?

    Equation: _____

67. 10 children are on the playground, 4 of them got hurt playing soccer. How many children were not hurt?

    Equation: _____

68. Put an X on dot "4E":

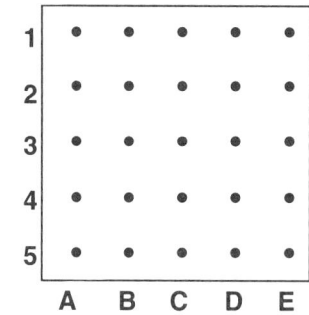

69. Put an Xs on dot "2B":

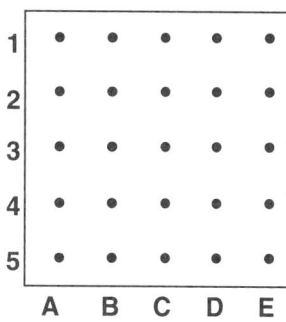

70. Which of these is a part of math? Circle the answer.
    a. patterns   b. numbers   c. shapes   d. all of these

GENERAL NATURE & USES OF MATHEMATICS

71. Can math be used to solve real-life problems?   Yes   No

72. Circle the things below that mean "12".

    a. 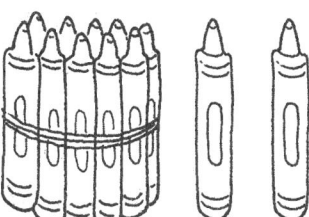   b. 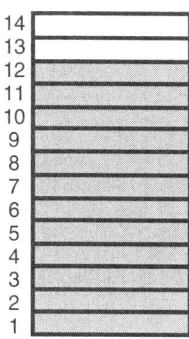   c. 11+1

End-of-Year Test Answer Key

1. April 9th
2. April 13th
3. December
4. 18 − 7 − 1 = 10 or
   18 − 8 = 10
5.

6. red
7. 17
8. 526
9. 89, 90, 91, 92
10. 68, 82, 149
11. 9 and 11
12. equal numbers:
    570 and 570
13. largest number:
    139
14. 68
15. 3 tens, 6 ones, 36
16. 16, 18, 20, 22, 24
17. 65, 70, 75, 80, 85
18. 60, 70, 80, 90, 100
19. Beth
20. even
21. 3
22. 3/6 or 1/2
23. 10
24. 3
25. 8
26. 2
27. 8
28. no
29. 2 inches
30. 1 inch
31. 3 centimeters
32. 2 centimeters
33. 5 centimeters
34. 3 centimeters
35. bear
36. 2 centimeters
37. the gallon
38. 3:00
39. 4:30
40. 70 degrees
41. a tape measure
42. 42 cents
43. 85 cents
44.
45.
46.
47.
48.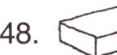
49.
50.
51. 4 sides
52. 8 sides
53. 4 sides
54. 5 sides
55. Students should draw a circle.
56. Students should color the second line.
57. Students should draw a vertical line down the center.
58.
59. 8
60. 6
61. orange juice
62. a. Amy's toss
63. a. 98 heads and 2 tails
65. Students should draw a colored circle.
64. b. ABC
66. 3 + 20 = 23 days
67. 10 − 4 = 6
68.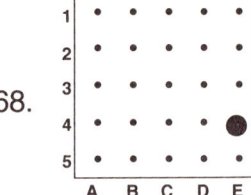
69.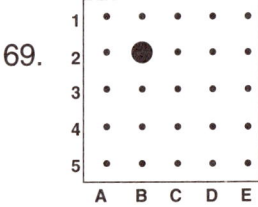
70. d. all of these
71. Yes
72. Students should circle all three pictures.

Add 0 - 3 | Subtract 0 - 3

Add 0 - 3		Subtract 0 - 3	
1+0	3+0	2-1	3-3
0+3	2+1	2-0	3-2
0+2	2+0	1-1	3-1
0+1	1+2	1-0	3-0
0+0	1+1	0-0	2-2

Add 4	Subtract 4	Add 4	Subtract 4
4+0	4-4	4+0	4-4
3+1	4-3	3+1	4-3
2+2	4-2	2+2	4-2
1+3	4-1	1+3	4-1
0+4	4-0	0+4	4-0

Add 5		Subtract 5	
4+1		5-4	
3+2		5-3	
2+3		5-2	
1+4		5-1	
0+5	5+0	5-0	5-5

Add to 6		Subtract from 6	
5+1	0+6	6−5	6−0
6+0	1+5	6−6	6−1
	2+4		6−2
	3+3		6−3
	4+2		6−4

Add to 7		Subtract from 7	
5+2	0+7	7-5	7-0
6+1	1+6	7-6	7-1
7+0	2+5	7-7	7-2
	3+4		7-3
	4+3		7-4

Add to 8 | Subtract from 8

Add to 8	Subtract from 8
5+3	8−0
6+2	8−1
7+1	8−2
8+0	8−3
0+8	8−4
1+7	8−5
2+6	8−6
3+5	8−7
4+4	8−8

Add to 9		Subtract from 9	
5+4	0+9	9-5	9-0
6+3	1+8	9-6	9-1
7+2	2+7	9-7	9-2
8+1	3+6	9-8	9-3
9+0	4+5	9-9	9-4

Add to 10		Subtract from 10	
4 + 6	0 + 10	10 − 5	10 − 10
5 + 5	1 + 9	10 − 4	10 − 9
7 + 3	2 + 8	10 − 3	10 − 8
8 + 2	3 + 7	10 − 2	10 − 7
9 + 1	6 + 4	10 − 1	10 − 6

Math Packs Answer Key

Math Pack 1

Patterns of One, p.12
Checkerboard pattern, star pattern, crayon pattern; ball and jacks are not in a pattern

Number Problem, p.13
0 + 1 = 1

Coin-Toss Addition, p.13
Coin toss will vary;
1 + 0 = 1; Answers will vary

Number Puzzle, p. 14
Answers will vary

The Classroom Store, p. 14
The teddy bear; 1 + 0 = 1; one penny

Telling Time, p. 15
Answers will vary

Tile Subtraction, p. 16
1: 1 − 1 = 0

Using a Calculator, p. 16
Add: 0, 1, 1,   Subtract: 0, 0, 1

Fractions, p. 17
Color shapes 1, 2, 5, 6, 7, and 8

Story Problems, p. 18
1: 1; 2: 0

Shape Study, p. 19
Color first butterfly, second heart, lightbulb, snowflake; drawings should show other half

Graphing, p. 20
60, 90, 20, 0, 70, 30, 80, 50; circle thermometers that show 20, 0, and 30.

Measuring Length, p. 21
Answers will vary

Measuring Volume, p. 22
4, 2, 2, 12, 3

Math Pack 2

Patterns of Two, p. 24
1: Answers will vary
2: Numbers will be colored in using an AB pattern of red and blue

Number Problem, p. 25
Answers will vary

Coin-Toss Addition, p. 25
Answers will vary

Number Puzzle, p. 26
Answers will vary

The Classroom Store, p. 26
The ball; answers will vary; two pennies

Telling Time, p. 27
2:00, 3:00, 4:00, 5:00, answers will vary

Tile Subtraction, p. 28
Answers will vary

Using a Calculator, p. 28
Add: 2, 2, 1, 1
Subtract: 0, 1, 0, 2

Fractions, p. 29
2/2 matches triangle, 2/3 matches circle, 2/12 matches rectangle; color 1/2 circle, color the whole rectangle

Story Problems, p. 30
1: 1, 2: 2

Shape Study, p. 31
No, you can't make shapes with zero sides on a geoboard

Sorting and Graphing, p. 32
Answers will vary

Measuring Length, p. 33
Answers will vary

Measuring Volume, p. 34
2, 2, 2, answers will vary

Math Pack 3

Patterns of Three, p. 36
1: c, d, p, c, d, p,
    d, h, c, d, h, c
    p, d, h, p, d, h
2: answers will vary
3: answers will vary

Number Problem, p. 37
Answers will vary

Coin-Toss Addition, p. 37
Answers will vary

Pattern Block Design, p. 38
3, answers will vary

Number Puzzle, p. 39
Answers will vary

The Classroom Store, p 39
The book, or the ball and teddy bear; answers will vary; three pennies

Tile Subtraction, p. 40
Answers will vary

Using a Calculator, p. 40
Add: 3, 3, 2, 3
Subtract: 0, 1, 3, 2

Coin-Toss Subtraction, p. 41
Answers will vary

Fractions, p. 42
1/3 of triangle, 2/3 of circle, 2 fish, 0 baseballs, 1 apple, 3 turtles

Story Problems, p. 43
1: 1, 2: 3, 3: 0

Shape Study, p. 44
Answers will vary

Telling Time, p. 45
3:00, 6:00, 9:00, 12:00; answers will vary

Sorting and Graphing, p. 46
Answers will vary

Measuring Length, p. 47
Answers will vary

Measuring Volume, p. 48
3, 3, color milk red, color flour red, color baking soda blue, color corn oil red

Math Pack 4

Patterns of Four, p. 50
Answers will vary; four

Number Problem, p. 51
Answers will vary

Coin-Toss Addition, p. 51
Answers will vary

Heads or Tails?, p. 52
Answers will vary

Pattern Block Design, p. 53
4, answers will vary

Number Puzzle, p 54
Answers will vary

The Classroom Store, p. 54
Dinosaur toy, or book and teddy bear; answers will vary; four pennies

Tile Subtraction, p. 55
Answers will vary

Coin-Toss Subtraction, p. 55
Answers will vary

Telling Time, p. 56
4:00, 4:30, answers will vary

Using a Calculator, p. 56
Add: 4, 4, 3, 4, 4, 0
Subtract: 1, 2, 4, 1, 1, 3

Fractions, p. 57
1/4 of the circle, 2/4 of the triangle, 3 trumpets, 4 drums, 0 pianos

Story Problems, p. 58
1: 2, 2: 4, 3: 3

Shape Study, p. 59
Answers will vary

Graphing, p. 60
Answers will vary

Measuring Length, p. 61
2, 1, 2, 1

Measuring Volume, p. 62
4, 12; jar filled with cups of water; answers will vary

Math Pack 5

Patterns of Five, p. 64
Counting by 5s; answers will vary

Number Problem, p. 65
Answers will vary

Coin-Toss Addition, p. 65
Answers will vary

Heads or Tails?, p. 66
Answers will vary

Pattern Block Design, p. 67
5, answers will vary

Number Puzzle, p. 68
Answers will vary

The Classroom Store, p. 68
The cup, or the book and ball, or the dinosaur and the teddy bear; answers will vary; the nickel

Tile Subtraction, p. 69
Answers will vary

Coin-Toss Subtraction, p. 69
Answers will vary

Telling Time, p. 70
5:00, 5:30

Using a Calculator, 70
Add: 5, 4, 5, 4, 5, 5
Subtract: 1, 1, 4, 0, 2, 5

Fractions, p. 71
1/5 of the circlt, 4/5 of the rectangle, 3 ants, 2 spiders, 0 bees, 5 worms

Story Problems, p. 72
1: 3, 2: 5, 3: 2

Shape Study, p. 73
Answers will vary

Graphing, 74
Answers will vary

Measuring Length, p. 75
Answers will vary

Measuring Perimeter, p. 76
4, 8, 12

Math Pack 6

Patterns of Six, p. 78
1: red, orange, yellow, green, blue, violet
2: orange, green, violet

Number Problem, p. 79
Answers will vary

Coin-Toss Addition, p. 80
Answers will vary

Heads or Tails?, p. 81
Answers will vary

Pattern Block Design, p. 82
6, answers will vary

Number Puzzle, p. 83
Answers will vary

The Classroom Store, 83
Box of crayons, or dinosaur toy and ball, or cup and teddy bear; answers will vary; a nickel and a penny

Tile Subtraction, p. 84
Answers will vary

Coin-Toss Subtraction, p. 85
Answers will vary

Telling Time, p. 86
6:00, 6:30, answers will vary

Using a Calculator, p. 86
Add: 6, 6, 5, 4, 6, 6, 5, 4, 6, 3, 6; Subtract: 1, 3, 4, 1, 1, 0, 2, 1, 6, 2, 5

Fractions, p. 87
5/6 of the circle, 3/6 of the triangle, 6 giraffes, 2 hippos, 4 zebras

Story Problems, p. 88
1: 6, 2: 4, 3: 1

Shape Study, p. 89
Answers will vary

Graphing, p. 90
Answers will vary

Measuring Length, p. 91
2, 3, 6, 4, 4, 8, 5, 3

Measuring Perimeter, p. 92
6, 10, 14

Math Pack 7

Patterns of Seven, p. 94
1: January, 2: 31, 3: 7, 4: 14, 5: Thursday, 6: 8, 7: 4, 8: 30, answers will vary

Number Problem, p. 95
Answers will vary

Coin-Toss Addition, p. 96
Answers will vary

Heads or Tails?, p. 97
Answers will vary

Pattern Block Design, p. 98
7, answers will vary

Number Puzzle, p. 99
Answers will vary

The Classroom Store, p. 99
The puzzle, or the box of crayons and the teddy bear, or the cup and the ball, or the dinosaur toy and the book, or the dinosaur toy, the ball, and the teddy bear, answers will vary, a nickel and two pennies

Tile Subtraction, p. 100
Answers will vary

Coin-Toss Subtraction, p. 101
Answers will vary

Telling Time, p. 102,
7:00, 7:30, answers will vary

Using a Calculator, p. 102
Add: 7, 7, 6, 7, 7, 6, 6, 7, 5, 5
Subtract: 1, 0, 3, 2, 1, 4, 7, 2, 1, 5

Fractions, p. 103
1/7 of the candy, 4/7 of the candy, no, the bread only has 7 slices, 7 bananas, 3 jars

Story Problems, p. 104
1: 2, 2: 6, 3: 7

Shape Study, p. 105
Answers will vary

Graphing, p. 106

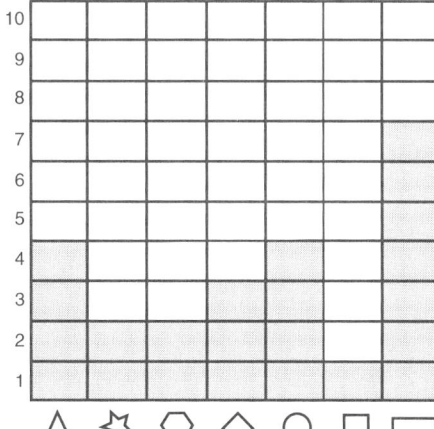

the rectangle

Measuring Length, p. 107
11, 10, 12, 9

Measuring Perimeter, p. 108
3, 6, 12

Math Pack 8

Patterns of Eight, p. 110
1: answers will vary
2: white and black, answers will vary, answers will vary, answers will vary

Number Problem, p. 111
Answers will vary

Coin-Toss Addition, p. 112
Answers will vary

Heads or Tails?, p. 113
Answers will vary

Pattern Block Design, p. 114
8, answers will vary

Number Puzzle, p. 115
Answers will vary

The Classroom Store, p. 115
The toy car, or the puzzle and the teddy bear, or the crayons and the ball, or the cup and the book, or the dinosaur toy, the book, and the teddy bear, or the cup, the ball, and the teddy bear, answers will vary, a nickel and three pennies

Tile Subtraction, p. 116
Answers will vary

Coin-Toss Subtraction, p. 117
Answers will vary

Telling Time, p. 118
8:00, 8:30, answers will vary

Using a Calculator, p. 118
Add: 8, 8, 8, 7, 8, 7, 8, 8, 8, 8, 8, 7, 7, 7, 4 Subtract: 1, 5, 4, 1, 8, 6, 3, 1, 2, 2, 2, 1, 0, 2, 7

Fractions, p. 119
1/8 of the circle, 6/8 of the square, 4 suns, 8 stars, 2 moons, 3 planets

Story Problems, p. 120
1: 6, 2: 8, 3: 5

Shape Study, p. 121
Answers will vary

Graphing, p. 122
Answers will vary

Measuring Length, p. 123
1: 4 inch wall, 2: roofs will vary, 3: door is 2 inches tall and wide 4: window is 1 inch tall and 3 inches wide 5: window is 1 inch long and 1 inch wide 6: decorations will vary

Measuring Volume, p. 124
8, 8, 1 cup, 1/2 cup, 1/2 teaspoon

Math Pack 9

Patterns of Nine. p. 126
1: patterns of nine, 2: 27, 36, 45, 54, 63, 72, 81, 90, numbers are the same

Number Problem, p. 127
Answers will vary

Coin-Toss Addition, p. 128
Answers will vary

Heads or Tails?, p. 129
Answers will vary

Pattern Block Design, p. 130
9, answers will vary

Number Puzzle, p. 131
Answers will vary

The Classroom Store, p. 131
The magnet, or the toy car and the teddy, or the puzzle and the ball, or the crayons and the book, or the cup and the dinosaur, or the crayons, ball and teddy bear, or the cup, book and teddy bear, or the dinosaur, book and ball; answers will vary; a nickel and 4 pennies

Tile Subtraction, p. 132
Answers will vary

Coin-Toss Subtraction, p. 133
Answers will vary

Telling Time, p. 134
8:30, 10:00, answers will vary

Using a Calculator, p. 134
Add: 9, 9, 8, 8, 9, 9, 9, 7, 9, 9
Subtract: 2, 7, 3, 2, 8, 4, 5, 1, 6, 2,

Fractions, p. 135
9/9, 3/9 + 2/9 + 4/9 = 9/9

Story Problems, p. 136
1: 2, 2: 9, 3: 6

Shape Study, p. 137
Answers will vary

Graphing, p. 138
Answers will vary

Measuring Length, p. 139
Answers will vary

Measuring Perimeter, p. 140
10, 16

Math Pack 10

Patterns of Ten, p. 142
1: Patterns of 10
2: answers will vary
   (fingers, toes, etc)

Number Problem, p. 143
Answers will vary

Coin-Toss Addition, 144
Answers will vary

Heads or Tails?, p. 145
Answers will vary

Pattern Block Design, p. 146
10, answers will vary

Number Puzzle, p. 147
Answers will vary

The Classroom Store, p. 147
The calculator, or the magnet and the teddy bear, or the car and the ball, or the puzzle and the book, or the crayons and the dinosaur toy, or the cup, the dinosaur toy, and the teddy bear, or the cup, the book, and the ball, or the dinosaur toy, the book, the ball, and the teddy bear; answers will vary; the dime or the nickel and five pennies

Tile Subtraction, p. 148
Answers will vary

Coin-Toss Subtraction, p. 149
Answers will vary

Telling Time, p. 150
10:00, 10:30, answers will vary

Using a Calculator, p. 150
Add: 10, 9, 9, 10, 10, 10, 8, 8, 10, 10 Subtract: 3, 9, 1, 7, 5, 4, 3, 3, 1, 0

Fractions, p. 151
2/10, 6/10, 2/10, 6/10, 7/10

Story Problems, 152
1: 8, 2: 10, 3: 5

Shape Study, p. 153
Answers will vary

Graphing, p. 154
5 pennies equal 5 cents, one nickel equals 5 cents, 10 pennies equal 10 cents, 2 nickels equal 10 cents, one dime equals 10 cents, 25 pennies equal 25 cents, 5 nickels equal 25 cents, one quarter equals 25 cents

Measuring Length, p. 155
Answers will vary

Measuring Volume, p. 156
1: 4 students, 2: 8 students, 3: 6 students